健康素

Simply Vegetarian

作　　者	林麗華
翻譯顧問	葛潔輝
出 版 者	純青出版社有限公司
	台北市松江路125號5樓
	郵政劃撥12106299
	電話：(02)5084331　傳真：(02)5074902
著作財產權人	財團法人味全文化教育基金會
版權所有	局版台業字第3884號
	中華民國85年11月初版發行
印　　刷	中華彩色印刷廠股份有限公司
定　　價	新台幣參佰元整

Author	Lee Hwa Lin
Translation Consultant	Connie Wolhardt
Publisher	Chin Chin Publishing Co., Ltd.
	5th fl., 125, Sung Chiang Rd.,
	Taipei, Taiwan, R.O.C.
	TEL:(02)5084331, FAX:(02)5074902
Distributor	Wei-Chuan Publishing
	1455 Monterey Pass Rd., #110
	Monterey Park, Ca 91754, U.S.A.
	TEL:(213)2613880 . 2613878
	FAX:(213)2613299
Printer	China Color Printing Co., Inc.
	Printed in Taiwan, R.O.C.
Copyright Holder	Copyright ©1997
	By Wei-Chuan Cultural Educational Foundation
	First Printing, Feb., 1997
	ISBN 0-941676-71-4

序

　　現代人追求健康，喜歡吃素的人愈來愈多，但是宗教的純素食限制嚴格，常使老饕望之怯步，針對這點，我們推出色香味俱全的「健康素」食譜，一方面滿足健康吃素的需求，另方面兼顧口腹之慾的生活享受。

　　自民國七十七年本會率先出版「素食」食譜後，許多健康素食者希望我們能繼續研究出版另一種與宗教無關、尺度較寬、變化較多的素食，經過一年的研究，味全家政班終於出版了這本「健康素」。

　　本書的菜餚，具有三大特色：
(1)菜色的豐富性。我們突破過去一般素食只是將加工品做成素雞、素鵝、素食形態的狹隘格局，拓展烹調領域，借助多元化的烹飪手法與多樣化的調味品，將素材料烹調出無異葷味，甚至超越葷菜的人間珍品。
(2)口味的清淡性。以低鹽、低糖、低油為烹飪主軸，符合健康原則。
(3)素材的開擴性。由於無關宗教，在材料的選擇上，除了肉以外，可以採用蔥、薑、蒜等辛香料，延伸素食的調味空間，使素食更加美味。

　　這本「健康素」的出版，希望讓所有喜歡吃素的讀者，吃的安心、吃的美味、吃的健康。

Foreword

In the pursuit of health, more and more people are turning to vegetarian dishes. However, the tight restrictions of strict vegetarianism often discourages the long term continued practice due to the lack of a variety in taste. We are now presenting an exciting cookbook, "Simply Vegetarian", which will meet both vegetarian needs and yet provide palatable enjoyment to the gourmet.

Since the publication of "Vegetarian Cooking" in 1988, we have received numerous warm responses from readers urging us to offer a less restrictive vegetarian cookbook with more variety. Accordingly, after one year of extensive research by the Wei Chuan Cooking School, "Simply Vegetarian" was created.

This new book possesses three unique characteristics:
(1) The extensive variety of tasty dishes provides a breakthrough in the narrow, traditional vegetarian food processing structure. With the provision of various cooking methods and spices, vegetarian dishes easily satisfy the need for a "Meaty Taste".
(2) Clarity of the taste. With low sodium, low sugar and low fat as the axis, all recipes fit perfectly within the principles of health.
(3)The expanded use of ingredients offers a broader and more liberal approach to vegetarian cooking, enhancing the taste of each dish.

With the publication of "Simply Vegetarian" , we wish all our readers a healthy and happy life, enhanced by delicious and healthy cooking.

Lee Hwa Lin

目錄 · Contents

5

高湯的製作 · Stock Preparation

葷高湯:
1 以豬、牛、雞的肉或骨（圖一）入開水中川燙。
2 再將肉或骨頭取出洗淨（圖二）。
3 以另一鍋水燒開後，再入洗淨的肉或骨頭，並加少許
　蔥、薑、酒（圖三）慢火熬出來的湯，謂之高湯。

Regular Stock :
1 Parboil pork, beef, chicken or bones (illus.1) in boiling water briefly.
2 Remove the meat or bones from the water and wash (illus.2).
3 Bring new clean water to a boil, add meat or bones together with a little green onion, ginger root, and cooking wine (illus.3). Turn the heat to high until the water is boiling, then turn the heat to low, simmer over low heat until the soup is tasty.

素高湯:一般分為紅燒用素高湯及清炒用素高湯
1 紅燒素高湯
　以香菇頭（圖一）、黃豆芽（圖二）、胡蘿蔔皮、白蘿
　蔔皮、大白菜的老葉及水熬成的湯，再過濾（圖三）即
　為紅燒素高湯。
2 清炒用素高湯
　大白菜的老葉、黃豆芽、胡蘿蔔皮、白蘿蔔皮、芹菜葉
　及水熬成之湯，再過濾即為清炒素高湯。

Vegetarian Stock:
There are two ways of making vegetarian stock dishes.
1 Stock to be used in soy-simmered dishes:
　Add dried black mushroom stems (illus.1), soy bean sprouts (illus.2), carrot and turnip peelings, and the outer leaves of cabbage in a pot with the water. Bring to a boil, then turn the heat low, simmer until the soup is tasty, remove all ingredients in the soup and strain the broth (illus.3).
2 Stock to be used for stir-fry dishes :
　Add the outer leaves of cabbage, soy bean sprouts, carrot and turnip peelings and celery leaves in a pot with the water. Bring to a boil, then turn the heat low, simmer until the soup is tasty, remove all the ingredients in the soup and strain the broth.

1b . = pound   g = gram   oz . = ounce

1兩 = 38公克 = 38g = $\frac{1}{12}$ lb . = $1\frac{1}{3}$ oz .

2兩 = 75公克 = 75g = $\frac{1}{6}$ lb . = $2\frac{2}{3}$ oz .

3兩 = 113公克 = 113g = $\frac{1}{4}$ lb . = 4 oz .

4兩 = 150公克 = 150g = $\frac{1}{3}$ lb . = $5\frac{1}{4}$ oz .

6兩 = 225公克 = 225g = $\frac{1}{2}$ lb . = 8 oz .

8兩 = 300公克 = 300g = $\frac{2}{3}$ lb . = $10\frac{1}{2}$ oz .

10兩 = 375公克 = 375g = $\frac{5}{6}$ lb . = $13\frac{1}{6}$ oz .

12兩 = 450公克 = 450g = 1 lb . = 16 oz .

16兩 = 600公克 = 600g = $1\frac{1}{3}$ lb . = 21 oz . = 1斤

量器介紹 · **Conversion Table**

1 杯
1 Cup = 1C . = 236 c.c.

1 大匙(1 湯匙)
1 Tablespoon = 1T . = 15 c.c.

1 小匙(1 茶匙)
1 Teaspoon = 1t . = 5c.c.

紅燒素獅子頭 · Mock Lion's Head

大白菜	450公克	**1**┌醬油	1大匙	
馬鈴薯	280公克	└味精	¹/₈小匙	
熟筍	28公克	**2**┌高湯	1杯	
香菇	2朵	│醬油	1大匙	
油條	1條	│糖	¹/₂小匙	
麵粉	¹/₃杯	└味精	¹/₈小匙	
太白粉	1大匙			

1 lb.(450 g) .... nappa cabbage	¹/₃ C. .... flour		
10 oz.(280 g)potatoes	1 T. .... cornstarch		
1 oz.(28 g) .... boiled bamboo shoots	**1** ┌ 1 T. ..... soy sauce		
2 .... dried black mushrooms	**2** ┌ 1 C. .... stock		
1 stick .... Chinese cruller	│ 1 T. ..... soy sauce		
	└ ¹/₂ t. .... sugar		

1 馬鈴薯洗淨連皮入開水中煮25分鐘,熄火續燜10分鐘後,撈起漂涼瀝乾,去皮壓粗碎;熟筍切細丁;油條切碎(圖一);香菇泡軟洗淨去蒂切小丁,泡香菇水2大匙留用;大白菜洗淨切大塊狀。

2 鍋熱入油2小匙燒熱,入香菇爆香,續入馬鈴薯、筍丁、油條、香菇水、**1**料及麵粉炒至麵粉被吸入後,盛起待涼,均分成4等份,每份搓成圓形,外表再沾上適量的太白粉即為素獅子頭。

3 鍋熱入油1¹/₂大匙燒熱,入獅子頭煎至兩面皆呈金黃色撈起,瀝油備用;另鍋熱入油1大匙燒熱,入大白菜炒數下,再加水¹/₂杯炒軟,熄火盛至砂鍋內,續入獅子頭及**2**料煮開,改小火續煮5分鐘即可。

1 Wash potatoes and boil for 25 minutes, turn off the heat and let stand covered for an additional 10 minutes. Remove and rinse under cold water to cool; drain. Peel off the skins and roughly crush the potatoes with a fork. Dice the bamboo shoots. Mince Chinese cruller (illus.1). Soak dried black mushrooms in warm water until soft, wash and remove the stems; dice. Retain 2 T. of the mushroom soaking water for later use. Wash nappa cabbage and cut into large serving pieces.

2 Heat a wok, add 2 t. oil and heat. Stir-fry diced black mushroom until fragrant. Add potatoes, diced bamboo shoots, Chinese cruller, black mushroom water, **1**, and flour. Stir-fry until flour is completely absorbed. Remove and leave to cool. Form the mixture into four balls, dust with cornstarch.

3 Heat a wok, add 1¹/₂ T. oil and heat. Fry the balls until the color turns golden brown on all sides. Remove and drain. In a clean wok, add 1 T. oil and heat. Stir-fry nappa cabbage and add ¹/₂ C. water; cook until tender. Remove the nappa cabbage to a casserole, place the balls on top and add **2**. Bring to a boil, then turn the heat to low and simmer for 5 minutes. Serve in casserole.

1

黃金蝦球 · Vegetarian Shrimp Balls

馬鈴薯 200公克	┌ 麵粉 .... ¼杯		
花椰菜 150公克	1 ┤ 酒 1小匙		
胡蘿蔔 120公克	┤ 鹽 .... ¼小匙		
荸薺 55公克	└ 味精 .... ⅛小匙		
熟青豆仁 .... ¼杯	┌ 高湯 .... ¾杯		
太白粉 2大匙	2 ┤ 鹽、糖 .... 各½小匙		
咖哩粉 .... ½大匙	└ 味精 .... ⅛小匙		
	3 ┌ 水 2小匙		
	└ 太白粉 .... ½小匙		

7 oz.(200 g) potatoes	┌ ¼ C. .... flour	
⅓ lb.(150 g) .... cauliflower	1 ┤ 1 t. ..cooking wine	
4¼oz.(120 g) carrots	└ ¼ t. .... salt	
2 oz.(55 g) .... water chestnuts	┌ ¾ C. .... stock	
¼ C. .... cooked green peas	2 ┤ ½ t. each: salt, sugar	
2 T. .... cornstarch	┌ 2 t. .... water	
½ T. .. curry powder	3 ┤ ½ t. .... cornstarch	

1 胡蘿蔔洗淨去皮，馬鈴薯洗淨連皮與胡蘿蔔入開水中煮至熟透（約25分鐘），撈起漂涼，瀝乾水份；花椰菜洗淨去老纖維切小塊，荸薺去皮切末備用。

2 馬鈴薯撕去外皮，與胡蘿蔔一起壓碎，入 **1** 料及荸薺拌勻即為馬鈴薯泥。取½大匙馬鈴薯泥，沾少許太白粉搓圓，即為蝦球。

3 鍋熱入油2大匙燒熱，入蝦球煎至兩面呈金黃色撈起。鍋續入油1大匙燒熱，入咖哩粉炒香，再入 **2** 料及花椰菜煮開，改小火燜煮至花椰菜軟化，再入蝦球及青豆仁炒勻，最後以 **3** 料勾芡即可。

1 Wash and pare the carrots. Wash potatoes and boil with carrots until cooked (about 25 minutes). Remove and rinse under cold water to cool; drain. Wash cauliflower, remove tough fibers and cut into small sprigs. Peel off the skin and mince water chestnuts.

2 Peel off the potato skins and mash with carrots, add **1** and minced water chestnuts; mix well to a paste. Roll ½ T. paste into a ball and dust with cornstarch.

3 Heat a wok, add 2 T. oil and heat. Fry the balls until golden on both sides, remove and drain. Add 1 T. oil into the wok, stir-fry curry powder until fragrant. Add **2** and cauliflower, bring to a boil. Turn the heat to low and simmer until tender. Add the balls and green peas, mix well. Thicken with **3** and serve.

白菜捲 · Cabbage Rolls

大白菜	450公克		水	1杯
胡蘿蔔	45公克	**1**	鹽	1½小匙
香菇	15公克		柴魚粉	1小匙
薑絲	1大匙	**2**	水	1大匙
干瓢	180公分		太白粉	1小匙

1 香菇泡軟洗淨去蒂，胡蘿蔔洗淨去皮，均入「滷香蒟
  蒻」滷汁（見88頁）中滷10分鐘，撈起切粗絲。入白
  菜洗淨以完整之片狀入開水中川燙至軟，撈起漂涼並
  擠乾水份，干瓢泡軟備用。

2 大白菜葉攤開，上置胡蘿蔔、香菇（圖一），再由內
  向外捲成桶狀（圖二），兩端用干瓢綁緊（圖三）並
  從中一切為二，置於盤中備用。

3 鍋熱入油1大匙燒熱，入薑絲爆香，續入**1**料煮開，
  並以**2**料勾芡，取出淋在白菜捲上，再入鍋蒸10分鐘
  即可。

1 lb.(450 g) .... nappa cabbage		6'(180 cm) .... dried gourd shavings	
1²/₃oz.(45 g) carrots			1 C. .... water
½oz.(15 g) .... dried black mushrooms		**1**	1½ t. .... salt
1T. .... shredded ginger root			1 t. .... dashi
		2	1 T. .... water
			1 t. ..... cornstarch

1 Wash dried black mushrooms and soak in warm water until soft, discard the stems. Wash the carrots and pare the skins. Braise both in a sauce of Braised Shirataki (ref. P. 88) for 10 minutes. Remove and shred both. Wash the nappa cabbage, separate each leaf and parboil in boiling water until tender. Remove the nappa cabbage leaves from the boiling water and rinse under cold water to cool; squeeze out excess water. Soak the dried gourd shavings in the water until soft, remove from water.

2 Spread out the nappa cabbage leaves, place shredded carrots and shredded black mushrooms on top (illus. 1). Roll from the center out ward (illus. 2) to form a cylinder. Tighten the ends with dried gourd shavings (illus. 3). Cut each roll into halves and arrange on a plate.

3 Heat a wok, add 1 T. oil and heat. Stir-fry shredded ginger root until fragrant. Add **1** and bring to a boil, thicken with **2**. Pour the sauce over cabbage rolls, and steam in a steamer for 10 minutes. Serve.

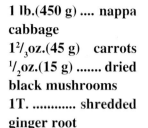

2

3

麵絲銀芽 · Delightful Mung Bean Sprouts

豆芽菜 300公克		┌ 紅辣椒 1條
麵腸 100公克	**1**	└ 蒜末、薑末 各1¹/₃小匙
酸菜 40公克		┌ 水 、醬油........各1大匙
鹽 .... ¹/₄小匙	**2**	│ 糖 1¹/₃小匙
		└ 胡椒粉 .... ¹/₈小匙

²/₃ lb.(300 g) ...... bean sprouts		┌ 1 red chili pepper
3¹/₂oz.(100 g) wheat gluten sausages	**1**	│ 1¹/₃ t. each:minced garlic cloves, │ minced ginger root
1¹/₃oz.(40 g) .... sour mustard	**2**	┌ 1 T. each: water, │ soy sauce │ 1¹/₃ t. .... sugar
¹/₄ t. .... salt		└ ¹/₈ t. .... pepper

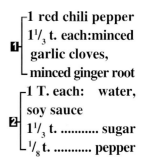

1 豆芽菜洗淨去頭尾（圖一），入水浸泡；麵腸切片再切成細絲，酸菜切絲（圖二），紅辣椒洗淨去籽切絲。

2 鍋熱入油1¹/₃大匙燒熱，入麵腸炒至金黃色，再入**2**料燒乾即盛起；豆芽菜撈起瀝乾備用。

3 鍋熱入油2大匙燒熱，入**1**料及酸菜炒香，再入豆芽菜及鹽拌炒1～2分鐘，最後入麵腸拌炒均勻即可。

1 Wash the sprouts and snip off both ends (illus.1); soak in cold water. Slice the wheat gluten sausages and then shred. Shred sour mustard (illus.2). Remove the seeds and shred red chili pepper.

2 Heat a wok, add 1¹/₃ T. oil and heat. Stir-fry shredded wheat gluten sausages until golden. Add **2** and cook until the sauce is completely evaporated, remove. Drain the bean sprouts and pat dry.

3 Heat a wok, add 2 T. oil and heat. Stir-fry **1** and shredded sour mustard until fragrant. Add the bean sprouts and salt, fry for 1 to 2 more minutes. Mix in fried wheat gluten sausages and serve.

1

2

奶油菠菜 · Buttered Spinach

菠菜 600公克		┌ 鹽 .... ¹/₂小匙
奶油、蒜頭 各28公克	**1**	味精、黑胡椒粉 ......
香菇 2朵		└ .... 各¹/₄小匙
錫箔紙（90×30cm）1張		

1¹/₃ lb.(600 g)spinach
1 oz.(28 g)each:butter, garlic cloves
2 .... dried black mushrooms

1 sheet .... aluminum foil (90 × 30 cm or 3'3" × 1'3")

1 ┌ ¹/₂ t. .... salt
¹/₄ t. .... black
└ pepper powder

1 菠菜洗淨切3公分長段；蒜頭去皮切片；錫箔紙摺成袋子狀（圖一）；香菇泡軟洗淨去蒂，切絲備用。

2 鍋熱入油1大匙及奶油燒熱，入蒜片、香菇爆香後，熄火入菠菜及**1**料拌勻，再裝入袋內（圖二）將袋口摺緊，置於乾鍋上（圖三），以中火蓋上鍋蓋，加熱3分半鐘，取出搖晃使其均勻，再打開錫箔紙置盤即可。

■ 如有烤箱，可先將烤箱預熱至200℃（392℉），入裝好菠菜的錫箔袋烤3分半鐘，其他做法與上述相同。

1 Wash spinach and cut into 3 cm (1¹/₄") sections. Peel the skins off the garlic cloves and slice. Fold the aluminum foil into a pocket (illus.1). Soak the dried black mushrooms in warm water until soft, discard the stems and shred.

2 Heat a wok, add 1 T. oil and butter and heat. Stir-fry garlic slices and shredded black mushrooms until fragrant. Turn off the heat, then add spinach and **1**; mix all ingredients well. Pack the spinach mixture into the foil pocket (illus.2). Place the foil pocket in a clean wok (illus.3) and cover with a lid. Heat over medium heat for 3 minutes. Remove from the wok and shake the foil pocket to evenly mix the content. Place the foil pocket on a plate and open the top to serve.

■ Alternative method: Preheat the oven to 200 °C (392°F). Bake the spinach mixture in the foil pocket for 3¹/₂ minutes.

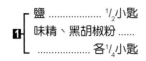

1

2

3

奶油焗花菜 · Cauliflower Au Gratin

花菜 580公克
起司絲 45公克
麵粉 .... ¹/₂杯
1┌ 水 5杯
　└ 鹽 1小匙

2 奶油、沙拉油各1大匙
3┌ 水 1¹/₄杯
　│ 奶水 3大匙
　│ 鹽 1小匙
　└ 糖、味精 ..... 各¹/₈小匙

20¹/₂oz.(580 g) ....
cauliflower
1²/₃oz.(45 g)shredded
cheese
¹/₂ C. .... flour
1┌ 5 C. .... water
　└ 1 t. .... salt

21 T. each: butter,
salad oil
3┌ 1¹/₄ C. .... water
　│ 3 T. .. evaporated
　│ milk
　│ 1 t. .... salt
　└ ¹/₈ t. .... sugar

1 烤箱預熱至200℃，花菜去老纖維切成小朵花狀洗淨。**1**料煮開後入花菜煮2～3分鐘，撈起瀝乾。

2 鍋熱入**2**料加熱至奶油完全融化，續入麵粉炒香，再慢慢入**3**料煮成濃稠麵糊，最後入花菜拌勻，即可盛入耐高溫之容器內，撒上起司絲，入烤箱烤至表面呈金黃色（約8～10分鐘）即可。

1 Preheat the oven to 200°C (392°F). Remove the tough fibers of cauliflower and cut into small serving sprigs; wash. Bring **1** to a boil and add cauliflower, boil for 2 to 3 minutes, remove and drain.

2 Heat a wok, add **2** and heat until butter melts. Add flour and fry until fragrant. Slowly add **3** and stir constantly to a thick paste. Mix in cauliflower evenly. Pour the mixture into a baking ceramic, sprinkle on shredded cheese and bake until golden on top (about 8 to 10 minutes). Serve.

燴高麗菜 ・ Wasabi Cabbage Rolls

高麗菜 450公克
1┌綠色芥末粉 2小匙
　└冷開水 1小匙
2┌醬油膏 3大匙
　└細砂糖 .... ¼小匙

1 lb.(450 g) cabbage
1┌ 2 t. wasabi powder
　│　(green mustard
　│　powder)
　└ 1 t. .... cold water
2┌ 3 T. ..... thick soy
　│　sauce
　│　¼ t. .. granulated
　└　sugar

1 **1**料調勻，再入**2**料混合拌勻即成沾料。
2 高麗菜洗淨，入開水中燙軟後撈起，入冷開水中漂涼，再置於竹簾上（圖一），密實地捲成（圖二）長桶狀，最後切成小段，食時沾料即可。

1 Mix **1** well, then mix with **2** to make the dipping sauce.
2 Wash the cabbage and parboil in boiling water until tender. Remove and rinse under cold water to cool. Place each leaf on the bamboo rolling sheet (illus.1), roll up tightly (illus.2) like a cylinder. Cut each roll into serving sections and serve with the dipping sauce on the side.

1　　2

燴雙色 · Savory Celery

西芹 500公克	
榨菜 20公克	
香菇 5朵	

1
水 1杯
酒 1大匙
鹽 1/2小匙
味精 .... 1/4 小匙

2
水 3大匙
太白粉 1/2大匙

1 西芹去老纖維後洗淨，切5公分長段，再切成條狀；入開水川燙後撈起漂涼；香菇洗淨泡軟去蒂切片；榨菜切薄片備用。
2 鍋熱入油2大匙燒熱，入榨菜爆香，續入香菇、西芹略炒，再入**1**料煮5分鐘，最後以**2**料勾芡即可。

17¹/₂oz.(500 g) celery
²/₃oz.(20 g) .... pickled
mustard head
5 .... dried black
mushrooms

1
1 C. .... water
1 T. cooking wine
1/2 t. .... salt

2
3 T. .... water
1/2 T. .. cornstarch

1 Remove the tough celery fibers, wash and cut into 5 cm (2") long sections, then cut into strips. Scald the celery in boiling water, remove and rinse under cold water. Wash dried black mushrooms, soak in warm water until soft; discard the stems and slice. Cut the pickled mustard head into thin slices.
2 Heat a wok, add 2 T. oil and heat ; stir-fry pickled mustard head slices until fragrant. Add black mushrooms and celery and fry. Pour in **1** and continue cooking for 5 minutes. Thicken with **2** and serve.

清炒雙脆 · Stir-fried Veggie Combination

四季豆 225公克	⎡鹽 .... ³/₄小匙
馬鈴薯 170公克	**1**⎢味精、胡椒粉 ....
胡蘿蔔絲、香菜末	⎣ .... 各¹/₈小匙
.... 各20公克	

8 oz.(225 g) ..... string beans
6 oz.(170 g) potatoes
²/₃oz.(20 g) each:
shredded carrots,
minced coriander

1⎡³/₄ t. .... salt
⎣¹/₈ t. .... pepper

1 馬鈴薯去皮切絲後泡水；四季豆亦洗淨切絲備用。
2 鍋熱入油2大匙燒熱，入馬鈴薯、四季豆略炒，再入胡蘿蔔絲及香菜末，最後入**1**料拌炒數下即可。

1 Pare off the skins and shred the potatoes; soak the shreds in water. Wash the string beans and shred.
2 Heat a wok, add 2 T. oil and heat. Stir-fry shredded potatoes and string beans briefly. Add shredded carrots and minced coriander and fry. Season with **1** and mix evenly. Serve.

金菇三絲 · Colorful Threads

金針菇	....	450公克
小黃瓜	....	125公克
胡蘿蔔	....	50公克
香菇	....	14公克

1
水	....	2大匙
酒	....	1大匙
鹽	....	$^1/_2$小匙
味精	....	$^1/_4$小匙
麻油	....	$^1/_8$小匙

1 lb.(450 g) .... golden mushrooms (enoki)
4$^1/_3$oz.(125 g) gherkin cucumbers
1$^3/_4$oz.(50 g) carrots
$^1/_2$oz.(14 g) .... dried black mushrooms

1
2 T. .... water
1 T. cooking wine
$^1/_2$ t. .... salt
$^1/_8$ t. .... sesame oil

1 香菇泡軟洗淨去蒂切絲；胡蘿蔔去皮切絲；小黃瓜亦洗淨切絲；金針菇（圖一）洗淨去頭，切段備用。
2 水4杯煮開，入金針菇川燙2分鐘後，撈起洗淨，瀝乾備用。
3 鍋熱入油2大匙燒熱，入香菇爆香，續入胡蘿蔔炒軟，再入金針菇及 **1** 料炒勻，最後入小黃瓜拌炒均勻即可。

1 Soak dried black mushrooms in warm water until soft, rinse and discard the stems; shred. Pare the carrots and shred. Wash the cucumbers and shred. Wash golden mushrooms (illus.1), trim off the ends and cut into sections.
2 Bring 4 C. water to a boil, scald golden mushrooms for 2 minutes. Remove and rinse; drain and pat dry.
3 Heat a wok, add 2 T. oil and heat. Stir-fry dried black mushrooms until fragrant. Add carrots and stir-fry until tender. Add golden mushrooms and **1**, stir-fry and mix well. Mix in cucumbers and serve.

1

金茸粉絲 · Enoki Noodles

金針菇（淨重） 220公克		┌ 高湯 1杯
香菇 37公克	**1**	醬油 1大匙
粉絲（圖一）...... 30公克		糖 1小匙
薑泥 1¹/₂大匙		└ 鹽 .... ¹/₂小匙
蔥末 1小匙		

7³/₄oz.(220 g) golden mushrooms (enoki)
1¹/₃oz.(37 g) ..... dried black mushrooms
1 oz.(30 g) .... bean threads (illus.1) (cellophane noodles)

1¹/₂ T. grated ginger root
1 t. ...... minced green onion

1
┌ 1 C. .... stock
1 T. ...... soy sauce
1 t. .... sugar
└ ¹/₂ t. .... salt

1 香菇泡軟洗淨去蒂切絲，金針菇（見22頁）洗淨去頭，入開水川燙至軟撈起，粉絲泡水5分鐘後切長段備用。

2 鍋熱入麻油2大匙燒熱，入香菇、薑泥爆香，續入金針菇及粉絲略炒再入 **1** 料燒煮至湯汁收乾，盛起撒上蔥末即可。

1 Soak dried black mushrooms in warm water until soft, discard the stems and shred. Wash golden mushrooms (ref. P. 22) and trim off the root ends; parboil in boiling water until tender, drain. Soak bean threads in water for 5 minutes and cut into long sections.

2 Heat a wok, add 2 T. sesame oil and heat. Stir-fry black mushrooms and grated ginger root until fragrant. Add golden mushrooms and bean threads, stir-fry briefly and season with **1** . Cook until all the sauce evaporates; remove onto a plate. Sprinkle on minced green onions and serve.

1

涼拌藕絲 · Lotus Root Salad

蓮藕 330公克
紫色高麗菜、胡蘿蔔 ......
.... 各30公克

┌蒜泥 10公克
│白醋 1大匙
1┤糖 1/₂大匙
│麻油 1小匙
└鹽 3/₄小匙

11¹/₂oz.(330 g) ....
.... lotus roots
**1 oz.(30 g) each: red
cabbage, carrots**

┌ **¹/₃oz.(10 g)** ....
│ **garlic paste**
1┤ **1 T. white vinegar**
│ **¹/₂ T.** .... **sugar**
│ **1 t. ..... sesame oil**
└ **³/₄ t.** .... **salt**

1 蓮藕洗淨去皮切絲，入開水中川燙1分鐘後取出，以
　冷水漂涼，撈起瀝乾備用。
2 胡蘿蔔洗淨去皮切細絲；紫色高麗菜洗淨亦切細絲備
　用。
3 將蓮藕、胡蘿蔔、紫色高麗菜及**1**料拌勻即可。

1 Wash the lotus roots, pare and shred. Scald
the roots in boiling water for 1 minute, rinse
under cold water; remove and pat dry.
2 Wash the carrots, pare and shred. Wash the
red cabbage and shred.
3 Toss the roots, carrots, red cabbage and **1**
together and serve.

蔥爆茭白筍 · Stir-fried Co-ba

茭白筍（圖一） 300公克	┌水 .... ½杯
胡蘿蔔 60公克	**1**├酒 1大匙
蔥 4枝	└鹽、味精 ..... 各¼小匙

$^2/_3$ lb.(300 g) ..... co-ba (illus.1)	┌$^1/_2$ C. .... water
2 oz.(60 g) ..... carrots	**1**├1 T. cooking wine
4 stalks green onion	└$^1/_4$ t. .... salt

1. 茭白筍洗淨切斜片；胡蘿蔔洗淨去皮亦切斜片；蔥洗淨切段備用。
2. 鍋熱入油2大匙燒熱，入蔥段爆香，續入胡蘿蔔、茭白筍拌炒數下，再入**1**料炒至湯汁收乾即可。

1 Wash co-ba and cut into diagonal slices. Wash the carrots, pare and cut into diagonal slices. Wash the green onions and cut into sections.
2 Heat a wok, add 2 T. oil and heat ; stir-fry the green onion sections until fragrant. Stir in carrot slices and co-ba and fry briefly. Add **1** and stir-fry until all the sauce is evaporated. Serve.

1

百合蘆筍 · Lily Bulbs and Asparagus

蘆筍 115公克	
百合、白果 各75公克	
香菇 3朵	

1
水 4大匙
鹽 1/2小匙
糖 1/4小匙
胡椒粉 1/8小匙

2
水 2小匙
太白粉 1/2小匙

$^{1}/_{4}$ lb.(115 g)............. asparagus
2 $^{2}/_{3}$ oz.(75 g) each: lily bulbs, ginkgo nuts
3............. dried black mushrooms

1
4 T. .... water
$^{1}/_{2}$ t. .... salt
$^{1}/_{4}$ t. .... sugar
$^{1}/_{8}$ t. .... pepper

2
2 t. .... water
$^{1}/_{2}$ t. ... cornstarch

1 白果（圖一）洗淨入鍋煮10分鐘，香菇泡軟洗淨去蒂切塊，蘆筍去老纖維洗淨切斜段，百合撥開（圖二）洗淨備用。

2 鍋熱入油2大匙燒熱，入香菇爆香，再入蘆筍、百合、白果及**1**料拌炒至熟，再以**2**料勾芡即可。

1 Wash the ginkgo nuts (illus.1) and steam for 10 minutes. Wash and soak dried black mushrooms in warm water until soft; discard the stem and cut into serving pieces. Remove the tough asparagus fibers, wash and cut into sections. Peel each petal off the lily bulbs (illus.2) and wash.

2 Heat a wok, add 2 T. oil and heat. Stir-fry the black mushrooms until fragrant. Add asparagus, lily bulb petals, ginkgo nuts and **1**, stir-fry until tender. Thicken with **2** and serve.

1   2

白果冬瓜 · Don Quia and Ginkgo Nuts

冬瓜（圖一）.... 850公克

1⎰ 香菇 28公克
⎱ 薑絲 10公克
⎱ 白果（見26頁）... 1罐

2⎰ 水 5杯
⎱ 醬油 3大匙
⎱ 冰糖 2大匙

30 oz.(850 g) ....
Don quia (illus.1)

1⎰ 1 oz.(28 g) dried
black mushrooms
$\frac{1}{3}$ oz.(10 g) ....
shredded ginger
root
1 can ginkgo nuts
(ref. P. 26)

2⎰ 5 C. .... water
⎱ 3 T. ..... soy sauce
⎱ 2 T. crystal sugar

1 冬瓜去皮及籽，香菇泡軟洗淨去蒂，切小塊備用。
2 鍋熱入油4大匙燒熱，入 **1** 料爆香，續入 **2** 料煮開，
再入冬瓜改小火煮至冬瓜熟爛（約80分鐘）後，取出
冬瓜切塊排盤，將 **1** 料置於中間並淋上剩餘湯汁即
可。

1 Pare the skins off Don quia and remove the
seeds. Soak dried black mushrooms in warm
water until soft, remove the stems and cut into
small pieces.
2 Heat a wok, add 4 T. oil and heat. Stir-fry all
ingredients in **1** until fragrant. Add **2** and bring
to a boil. Add Don quia. Simmer over low heat
until tender (about 80 minutes). Remove the
Don quia, cut into serving pieces and arrange
in a circle on a plate. Place **1** in the center and
pour on the remaining sauce. Serve.

1

黃金苦瓜 · Bitter Gourd Salad

苦瓜 180公克	黑胡椒粉、鹽............
洋菜（圖一）、金針（圖	.... 各½小匙
二）.................... 各10公克	味精、糖、白胡椒粉
酒 1大匙	.... 各⅛小匙
豆豉........................ ½大匙	

1（bracket grouping seasonings）

6⅓oz.(180 g) ...bitter gourd
⅓oz.(10 g)each:agar-agar (illus.1) , dried lily buds (illus.2)
1 T. ..... cooking wine
½ T. .... fermented black beans

1 ½ t. each: black pepper powder, salt
⅛ t. each: sugar, white pepper powder

1 苦瓜洗淨去籽切薄片，入開水中川燙，隨即撈起漂涼備用。
2 金針入水中泡軟後去頭打結，再入開水中川燙備用。
3 洋菜洗淨切4公分長段，泡冷開水至軟撈起，豆豉加酒泡軟備用。
4 鍋熱入麻油1大匙燒熱，入豆豉爆香，熄火入金針、洋菜、苦瓜及 **1** 料拌勻，置冰箱冷藏15分鐘即可。

1 Wash bitter gourd, remove the seeds and slice thin. Parboil in boiling water; remove and rinse under cold water to cool.
2 Soak dried lily buds in water until soft, remove the ends and tie into knots. Parboil in boiling water, remove and drain.
3 Wash agar-agar and cut into 4 cm (1½") sections; soak in cold water until soft, drain. Soak fermented black beans in cooking wine until soft.
4 Heat a wok, add 1 T. sesame oil and heat. Stir-fry fermented black beans until fragrant. Turn off the heat, then add lily buds, agar-agar, bitter gourd and season with **1**. Mix all ingredients well. Refrigerate for 15 minutes before serving.

1

2

芝麻牛蒡絲 · Sesame Gobo

牛蒡（圖一）.... 300公克
熟白芝麻 2大匙
麻油 1小匙

❶
酒 .... ¹/₂杯
糖 2大匙

❷
醬油 1¹/₂大匙
味精 .... ¹/₄小匙

$^{2}/_{3}$ lb.(300 g)................
burdock (illus.1)
2 T. ..... roasted white
sesame seeds
1 t. .... sesame oil

❶
¹/₂ C. cooking wine
2 T. .... sugar

❷ 1¹/₂ T. .... soy sauce

1 牛蒡洗淨去皮切細絲後，置水中備用。

2 鍋熱入油3大匙燒熱，入牛蒡略炒，再入 **❶** 料煮至湯汁剩¹/₄杯後，入 **❷** 料續炒至湯汁收乾，最後入麻油拌匀，盛盤時灑上芝麻即可。

1 Wash burdock and pare off the tough skin; shred. Soak the shreds in water.

2 Heat a wok , add 3 T. oil and heat. Stir-fry shredded burdock, then add **❶** and cook until the sauce is reduced to ¹/₄ C. . Add **❷** and stir-fry until all the sauce evaporates. Mix in sesame oil and remove. Sprinkle on sesame seeds and serve.

1

萵苣蘿蔔乾 · Daikon and Lettuce

西生菜 300公克
蘿蔔乾 70公克

1［高湯 .... ½杯
　 ［鹽、味精 .... 各½小匙

2［水 1大匙
　 ［太白粉 2小匙

1 蘿蔔乾洗淨剁碎，西生菜切片備用。
2 鍋熱入油2大匙燒熱，入蘿蔔乾略炒後盛起備用。
3 鍋熱入油1大匙燒熱，入西生菜及**1**料以大火快炒數下，再以**2**料勾芡，起鍋前入蘿蔔干拌勻即可。

10½oz.(300 g) ....
.... lettuce
2½oz.(70 g) .... salt-
preserved daikon

1［ ½ C. .... stock
　 ［ ½ t. .... salt

2［ 1 T. .... water
　 ［ 2 t. .... cornstarch

1 Wash and mince salt-preserved daikon. Cut the lettuce into serving pieces.
2 Heat a wok, add 2 T. oil and heat. Stir-fry minced salt-preserved daikon until fragrant and remove.
3 Heat a wok, add 1 T. oil and heat . Stir-fry lettuce and **1** over high heat for a while. Thicken with **2** . Mix in salt-preserved daikon and serve.

30

梅子醬瓜 · Cucumbers with Plum Sauce

小黃瓜 300公克	細砂糖 .... 2 大匙
紫蘇梅（圖一） 100公克	麻油 1小匙
紫蘇葉（圖二）........ 5片	

$^2/_3$ lb.(300 g) .... gherkin cucumbers
$3^1/_2$oz.(100 g) .... preserved sour plums (illus.1)

5 leaves .... perilla (illus.2)
2 T. granulated sugar
1 t. .... sesame oil

1 小黃瓜洗淨，入開水中川燙30秒撈起漂涼後，切成4長條，再切3公分段備用。

2 紫蘇梅去籽，連同紫蘇葉及細砂糖剁碎至糖溶化，再入麻油拌勻即為梅子醬。

3 食時將黃瓜沾梅子醬即可。

1 Wash gherkin cucumbers, parboil in boiling water for 30 seconds. Remove and rinse under cold water to cool. Cut each into 4 equal long strips, then into 3 cm ($1^1/_4$") sections.

2 Remove the pits from preserved sour plums. Chop plums, perilla and sugar together until sugar is dissolved. Mix in sesame oil evenly. This is the plum paste.

3 Serve the gherkin cucumbers with plum paste as dipping sauce.

1

2

沙茶鮮香菇 · Sa-tsa Mushrooms

新鮮香菇 250公克	┌ 醬油、沙茶醬 ....
胡蘿蔔、豌豆莢各75公克	**1** .... 各2 大匙
枸杞 1大匙	└ 鹽 .... ¹/₄小匙
蒜末 1小匙	

8³/₄oz.(250 g) ....fresh black mushrooms
2²/₃oz.(75 g) each: carrots, Chinese pea pods
1 T. ... lycium berries

1 t. ..... minced garlic cloves

1 ┌ 2 T. each:soy sauce, barbecue(sa-tsa) sauce
└ ¹/₄ t. .... salt

1 新鮮香菇（圖一）洗淨去蒂切成4等份入開水中川燙1分鐘撈起；胡蘿蔔切片，入開水中煮至軟，取出備用。

2 鍋熱入油1大匙燒熱，入蒜末及**1**料炒香，續入香菇炒熟後入胡蘿蔔、豌豆莢及枸杞（圖二）拌炒數下即可。

1 Wash the fresh black mushrooms (illus.1), discard the stems and cut each into quarters. Parboil the black mushrooms for 1 minute and remove. Slice the carrots and boil in water until tender; drain.

2 Heat a wok, add 1 T. oil and heat. Stir-fry minced garlic cloves and **1** until fragrant. Add the fresh black mushrooms and stir-fry until tender. Add carrot slices, Chinese pea pods and lycium berries (illus.2); stir to mix evenly and serve.

1

2

香菇紫菜 · Mushrooms with a Purple Touch

新鮮香菇 300公克
紫色高麗菜 85公克
豌豆莢 8片
蔥段 4段

1 ┌水 1/2杯
│麻油 1小匙
│鹽 1/4小匙
└味精 1/8小匙

2/3 lb.(300 g) ...... fresh
black mushrooms
3 oz.(85 g) .... red
cabbage
8 pieces .... Chinese
pea pod

4 sections .... green
onion

1 ┌1/2 C. .... water
│1 t. ...... sesame oil
└1/4 t. .... salt

1 新鮮香菇（見32頁）洗淨，入開水中川燙，隨即撈起漂涼去蒂切成片狀；紫色高麗菜洗淨撕成片狀；豌豆莢去頭尾亦斜切片狀備用。

2 鍋熱入油2大匙燒熱，入蔥段爆香，續入香菇、紫色高麗菜及**1**料煮約15分鐘後，再入豌豆莢炒熟即可。

1 Wash fresh black mushrooms (ref. P. 32), parboil in boiling water; remove immediately and rinse under cold water to cool. Remove the stems and slice the mushrooms. Wash the red cabbage and tear into serving pieces by hand. Trim off the ends of Chinese pea pods and cut in diagonal slices.

2 Heat a wok, add 2 T. oil and heat. Stir-fry green onion sections until fragrant. Add fresh black mushroom slices, red cabbage pieces and **1** to cook for 15 minutes. Mix in Chinese pea pods and cook until tender. Serve.

香菇四季豆 · Mushrooms and String Beans

四季豆 240公克
香菇 15公克
紅辣椒 1枝

┌ 水 2大匙
│ 酒 1大匙
1┤ 黑胡椒粉、鹽 ....
│ .... 各½小匙
└ 味精 .... ¼小匙

8½ oz.(240 g) string beans
½ oz.(15 g)dried black mushrooms
1 ..... red chili pepper

┌ 2 T. .... water
│ 1 T. cooking wine
1┤ ½ t. each: black
└ pepper powder,salt

1 將四季豆去頭尾切成1.5公分長的顆粒狀，入開水中川燙1分鐘，撈起漂涼；香菇泡軟洗淨去蒂切小丁，紅辣椒去籽切小丁備用。
2 鍋熱入油1大匙燒熱，入辣椒及香菇爆香，續入四季豆及 **1** 料以小火煮至湯汁收乾即可。冰涼後食之亦可。

1 Trim off the ends of string beans and cut into 1.5 cm (½") short tubes. Parboil the string beans in boiling water for 1 minute; remove and rinse under cold water to cool. Wash and soak the dried black mushrooms in warm water until soft, discard the stems and dice. Remove the seeds and dice the red chili pepper.
2 Heat a wok, add 1 T. oil and heat. Stir-fry red chili pepper and mushrooms until fragrant. Add string beans and **1** , simmer over low heat until all the sauce evaporates. Serve warm or cold.

香酥甜豆 · Sugar Snow Peas Salad

甜豆（圖一）.... 300公克	┌麻油 .... 1 小匙
菜酥（圖二）......... 2大匙	**1**┤黑胡椒粉、鹽 ....
八角 5粒	└ .... 各¹/₂小匙

10¹/₂oz.(300 g) sugar snow peas (illus.1)
2 T. .. vegetable crisp (tsai su)(illus.2)
5 pieces ..... star anise

┌**1 t. .... sesame oil**
1┤**¹/₂ t. each: black pepper powder,**
└**salt**

1 水4杯煮開，入八角煮10分鐘，續入甜豆燙熟（約5分鐘）撈起瀝乾，再入**1**料拌勻，待涼，最後入菜酥拌均即可。

1 Bring 4 C. water to boil, add star anise and cook for 10 minutes. Add sugar snow peas and boil until tender (about 5 minutes). Remove the pea pods and drain. Mix the pea pods with **1** and leave to cool. Mix in vegetable crisp (tsai su) and serve.

1   2   35

醋溜豇豆 • Long Bean Vinaigrette

長豇豆（圖一） 300公克	⌐水 1杯	
醬油 1大匙	**1**⊢糖 1小匙	
白醋 1小匙	⌐鹽 .... ¹/₂小匙	

10¹/₂oz.(300 g) ....
long beans (illus.1)
1 T. .... soy sauce
1 t. ..... white vinegar

⌐1 C. .... water
1⊢1 t. .... sugar
⌐¹/₂ t. .... salt

1 豇豆去頭尾洗淨，切成5公分段備用。
2 鍋熱入油2大匙燒熱，入豇豆拌炒數下，再由鍋邊入
  醬油炒香，隨即入 **1** 料以小火煮至湯汁收乾，起鍋前
  入白醋拌勻即可。

1 Trim off the ends and wash the long beans.
  Cut into 5 cm (2") sections.
2 Heat a wok, add 2 T. oil and heat. Stir-fry
  long beans slightly, add soy sauce and stir-fry
  until fragrant. Add **1** and simmer over low heat
  until the sauce completely evaporates. Mix in
  white vinegar and serve.

1

拌三丁 · Chive Salad

白豆干 150公克	┌麻油 4小匙
番茄 130公克	│糖 1小匙
韭菜 90公克 **1**	│鹽 .... ³/₄小匙
	└味精 .... ¹/₈小匙

$^1/_3$ lb.(150 g) .... white pressed bean curd
$4^1/_2$oz.(130 g)tomatoes
$3^1/_4$oz.(90 g) .... chives

┌4 t. ...... sesame oil
1 ┤1 t. .... sugar
└³/₄ t. .... salt

1 番茄洗淨去蒂及籽後，切小丁；白豆干切小丁（圖一）
　入鍋川燙；韭菜（圖二）亦入鍋川燙後，撈起漂涼，
　擠乾水份切小丁備用。
2 將所有材料及**1**料拌匀即可。

1 Wash the tomatoes, remove the stems and seeds; dice. Dice the pressed bean curd (illus.1) and scald in boiling water briefly then remove. Scald the chives (illus.2) in boiling water, remove and rinse under cold water; squeeze out water and dice.

2 Toss all ingredients and **1** well. Serve.

1

2

素拉皮 · Appetizer with Sesame Sauce

素火腿（圖一） 220公克
粉皮（圖二）.... 120公克
小黃瓜 100公克
辣油 .... ½大匙

1
┌ 醬油膏 3大匙
│ 芝麻醬 1½大匙
│ 麻油、高湯 各1大匙
│ 薑末、糖、蔥末、白
│ 醋、蒜末..... 各1小匙
│ 花椒粉 .... ½小匙
└ 味精 .... ¼小匙

7³/₄oz.(220 g) ....
vegetarian ham
(illus.1)
4¹/₄oz.(120 g) mung
bean sheets (illus.2)
3¹/₂oz.(100 g)gherkin
cucumbers
¹/₂ T. .... chili oil

1
┌ 3 T. thick soy sauce
│ 1¹/₂T. sesame paste
│ 1 T. each: sesame
│ oil, stock
│ 1 t. each: minced
│ ginger root, sugar,
│ minced green onion,
│ white vinegar,
│ minced garlic
│ cloves
│ ¹/₂ t. Szechwan pep-
└ ppercorn powder

1 素火腿、小黃瓜均切薄片，再切細絲；粉皮切粗條入
 開水中川燙後撈起，漂涼備用。
2 粉皮置盤，上置小黃瓜絲，最上面再放火腿絲，食時
 淋上拌勻之 **1** 料並灑上辣油即可。

1 Shred vegetarian ham and gherkin cucumbers
 into thin strips. Cut the mung bean sheets into
 thick strips and scald in boiling water; rinse
 under water to cool.
2 Arrange the mung bean strips on a plate, spread
 on shredded cucumbers. Then arrange shredded
 ham on top. Pour well-mixed **1** sauce on and
 sprinkle with chili oil. Serve.

1

2

棗香金寶 · Jujube Flavored Bean Curd Pouches

油炸豆包（圖一）	170公克
草菇	56公克
金針（見28頁）	20公克
薑絲	1大匙
紅棗	8個

1	水	½杯
	酒	1大匙
	糖	½小匙
	鹽	¼小匙
	味精	⅛小匙

6 oz.(170 g)fried bean curd pouches (illus.1)
2 oz.(56 g) .... straw mushrooms
²/₃oz.(20 g) dried lily buds (ref. P. 28)
8 .... red jujubes

1 T. .... shredded ginger root

1	½ C. .... water
	1 T. cooking wine
	½ t. .... sugar
	¼ t. .... salt

1 將豆包一切成四；金針泡軟洗淨後打結；紅棗（圖二）泡軟切開去籽；草菇切半入鍋川燙，撈起漂涼備用。

2 鍋熱入油1大匙燒熱，入薑絲爆香，續入草菇、金針、紅棗及 **1** 料煮至湯汁剩¼杯，再入豆包拌炒至湯汁剩1大匙即可。

1 Cut each fried bean curd pouch into quarters. Soak dried lily buds in water until soft, wash then tie into knots. Soak dried red jujubes (illus.2) until soft, cut open and remove the seeds. Cut each straw mushroom in half, scald in boiling water; remove and rinse under cold water to cool, drain.

2 Heat a wok, add 1 T. oil and heat ; stir-fry shredded ginger root until fragrant. Add straw mushrooms, lily buds, red jujubes, and **1** to cook until the sauce reduces to ¼ C. . Add fried bean curd pouches and stir to mix well; cook until the sauce reduces to 1 T. . Serve.

1

2

豆酥香豆腐 · Tofu with Crispy Soy Beans

嫩豆腐	1盒
蔥末	1¹/₂小匙
豆酥	28公克

1
水	¹/₂杯
鹽、糖	各¹/₄小匙
胡椒粉	¹/₈小匙

2
| 蔥末、薑末、蒜末 | 各1小匙 |
| 辣豆瓣醬 | ¹/₂小匙 |

3
| 水 | 1小匙 |
| 太白粉 | ¹/₂小匙 |

1 箱 .... soft tofu
1¹/₂ t.   minced green onion
1 oz. (28 g) .... beige fermented beans

1
| ¹/₂ C. .... water |
| ¹/₄ t. each:salt,sugar |
| ¹/₈ t. .... pepper |

2
| 1 t. each: minced green onion,minced ginger root,minced garlic cloves |
| ¹/₂ t. ..... chili bean paste |

3
| 1 t. .... water |
| ¹/₂ t. .... cornstarch |

1 嫩豆腐切成2×4公分長條狀,豆酥切末（圖一）。
2 鍋熱入油1大匙燒熱,入蔥末1小匙爆香,續入**1**料及豆腐,以小火燜煮10分鐘,再以**3**料勾芡取出置盤。
3 鍋熱入油2¹/₂大匙燒熱,入豆酥以小火炒至香酥,再入**2**料爆香,取出置於豆腐上並撒上蔥末即可。

1 Cut soft tofu into 2×4 cm (1"×1¹/₂") long strips. Chop beige fermented beans (illus.1) .
2 Heat a wok,add 1 T. oil and heat; stir-fry 1 t. minced green onion until fragrant. Add **1** and tofu, simmer over low heat for 10 minutes. Thicken with **3** and remove to a plate.
3 Heat a wok, add 2¹/₂ T. oil and heat; fry beige fermented beans until crispy. Add **2** and stir-fry until fragrant. Pour the bean mixture over the tofu. Sprinkle on minced green onion and serve.

1

蔥燒豆腐 · Green Onion Braised Tofu

豆腐 300公克	┌ 水 .... ½杯
蔥 120公克	**1** ┤ 醬油 2大匙
	└ 糖、味精 .... 各½小匙

10½oz.(300 g) ... tofu	┌ ½ C. .... water
4¼oz.(120 g) ...green	**1** ┤ 2 T. ...... soy sauce
onions	└ ½ t. .... sugar

1 在豆腐表面交叉切刀（圖一），深度至豆腐一半的厚度，蔥洗淨切3公分長段備用。
2 鍋熱入油3大匙燒熱，入蔥段爆香，再入**1**料及豆腐燒至湯汁快收乾即可。

1 Score tofu with diagonal cuts (illus.1) , as deep as half of the depth of the tofu. Wash green onions and cut into 3 cm (1¼") sections.
2 Heat a wok, add 3 T. oil and heat; stir-fry green onion sections until fragrant. Add **1** and tofu and simmer until the sauce is nearly evaporated. Serve.

1

酸菜油豆腐 · Sour Mustard and Tofu

四角油豆腐 225公克
熟筍、酸菜 各150公克
蒜末 1½大匙

1
┌ 水 1杯
│ 酒 2大匙
│ 醬油 1大匙
└ 糖 1小匙

8 oz.(225 g) fried bean
curd squares
5⅓oz.(150 g)each:
boiled bamboo shoots,
sour mustard
1½ T. minced garlic
cloves

1
┌ 1 C. .... water
│ 2 T. cooking wine
│ 1 T. ..... soy sauce
└ 1 t. .... sugar

1 油豆腐一切為6塊（圖一），筍切薄片，入鍋川燙5分
鐘後，撈起漂涼；酸菜洗淨切小丁備用。

2 鍋熱入油2大匙燒熱，入蒜末爆香，續入酸菜略炒，再
入筍、油豆腐及**1**料煮15分鐘即可。

1 Cut each fried bean curd square into six pieces
(illus.1). Slice the bamboo shoots, scald in
boiling water for 5 minutes; remove and rinse
under cold water to cool, drain. Wash the sour
mustard and chop fine.

2 Heat a wok, add 2 T. oil and heat; stir-fry
minced garlic cloves until fragrant. Add
chopped sour mustard and stir-fry for a little
while. Add bamboo shoot slices, fried bean
curd squares, and **1**, cook for 15 minutes.
Serve.

1

麻婆豆腐 · Ma Po Tofu

豆腐 360公克	水 2杯	
蒜苗 1枝	醬油 1大匙	
辣豆瓣醬 1¹/₃大匙	糖 2小匙	**2**
花椒粉 .... ¹/₂小匙	酒 1小匙	
1 蔥末 2大匙	味精 .... ¹/₂小匙	
蒜末 1大匙	鹽 .... ¹/₄小匙	
薑末 1小匙	水 1大匙	**3**
	太白粉 .... ¹/₂大匙	

12²/₃oz.(360 g) .... tofu
1 stalk ..... fresh garlic
1¹/₃ T. chili bean paste
¹/₂ t. .... Szechwan
peppercorn powder

1
2 T. minced green onion
1 T. minced garlic cloves
1 t. minced ginger root

2
2 C. .... water
1 T. ..... soy sauce
2 t. .... sugar
1 t. cooking wine
¹/₄ t. .... salt

3
1 T. .... water
¹/₂ T. .. cornstarch

1 豆腐切小丁，蒜苗洗淨切末備用。

2 鍋熱入油2大匙燒熱，入**1**料爆香，續入辣豆瓣醬炒香，再入**2**料及豆腐煮開，改小火續煮20分鐘後，以**3**料勾芡，最後入蒜苗末及花椒粉拌勻即可。

1 Dice the tofu. Wash fresh garlic and mince.

2 Heat a wok, add 2 T. oil and heat. Stir-fry **1** until fragrant. Add chili bean paste and stir-fry until fragrant. Add **2** and tofu, bring to a boil. Turn the heat to low and simmer for 20 minutes. Thicken with **3**. Mix in minced fresh garlic and peppercorn powder. Serve.

家常素肉乾 · Vegetarian Jerky

麵腸 200公克	┌ 水 .... ¹/₄杯
紅辣椒 1條	**1**├ 醬油 1大匙
熟芝麻 1大匙	└ 糖 1小匙

1 麵腸洗淨，用手撕成大小不等之片狀；紅辣椒亦洗淨去籽切斜片備用。

2 鍋熱入油2大匙燒熱，入辣椒爆香，再入麵腸炒至金黃色後，續入 **1** 料燒煮至湯汁剩1大匙時，取出盛盤並灑上芝麻即可。

7 oz.(200 g) ..... wheat gluten sausages
1 ..... red chili pepper
1 T. roasted sesame seeds

┌ ¹/₄ **C. ....** water
1├ **1 T. ......** soy sauce
└ **1 t . ...** sugar

1 Wash wheat gluten sausages, tear them by hand to irregular pieces. Wash the red chili pepper, remove the seeds and slice .

2 Heat a wok, add 2 T. oil and heat. Fry red chili pepper until fragrant. Add wheat gluten sausages, and fry until golden. Add **1** and cook until the sauce reduces to 1 T. . Remove from the wok and sprinkle on sesame seeds. Serve.

素火腿卷 · Vegetarian Ham Rolls

芥蘭菜 230公克		水 .... ¹/₂杯	
素火腿 180公克		酒 1大匙	
干瓢 140公克	**1**	醬油 2小匙	
熟筍絲 60公克		糖 .... ¹/₂小匙	
蔥絲 30公克		味精 .... ¹/₈小匙	
麻油 .... ¹/₂小匙			

¹/₂ lb.(230 g) gai lan	1 oz.(30 g) shredded
6¹/₃ oz.(180 g)	green onions
vegetarian ham	¹/₂ t. .... sesame oil
5 oz.(140 g) ...... dried	¹/₂ C. .... water
gourd shavings	1 T. cooking wine
2 oz.(60 g) shredded	2 t. .... soy sauce
boiled bamboo shoots	¹/₂ t. .... sugar

1 素火腿（見38頁）切12片；干瓢泡軟切成12段（圖一）。

2 芥蘭菜洗淨切兩段後，用開水燙熟撈起漂涼排盤。

3 每片素火腿上置筍絲、蔥絲（圖二），再包捲成圓桶狀，用干瓢綁緊即為素火腿卷。

4 鍋熱入油1大匙燒熱，入素火腿卷及**1**料煮開後改小火煮至湯汁收乾（約5分鐘），撒上麻油，置於芥蘭菜上即可。

1 Cut vegetarian ham (ref. P. 38) into 12 slices. Soak dried gourd shavings until soft and cut into 12 strings (illus.1).

2 Wash gai lan and cut in half. Parboil in boiling water and rinse under cold water to cool, drain. Arrange gai lan on a plate.

3 Place a portion of the shredded bamboo shoots and shredded green onions on a slice of ham (illus.2) and roll up as a cylinder. Tie each roll with a dried gourd shaving.

4 Heat a wok, add 1 T. oil and heat . Add vegetarian ham rolls and **1**, bring to a boil. Turn the heat to low and simmer until the sauce evaporates (about 5 minutes). Sprinkle on sesame oil. Arrange the rolls over gai lan and serve.

1

2

香酥豆包 · Stuffed Tofu Pouches

香菜	60公克		胡椒粉	³/₄小匙
豆包	6片	**1**	鹽	¹/₂小匙
			糖	¹/₄小匙

2 oz.(60 g) coriander			³/₄ t.	pepper
6 pieces .... bean curd pouches		**1**	¹/₂ t.	salt
			¹/₄ t.	sugar

1 香菜洗淨切碎，**1**料調勻，兩者均分成6等份備用。

2 將豆包攤開，均勻抹上**1**料（圖一），再將香菜置於其上（圖二）並將豆包折回原狀。

3 鍋熱入油2大匙燒熱，入豆包煎至兩面呈金黃色，取出切塊即可。

1 Wash and mince coriander. Mix **1** well. Divide both into 6 equal portions.

2 Spread out bean curd pouches, evenly brush each pouch with one portion of **1** (illus.1) and sprinkle on one portion of coriander (illus.2). Fold the pouches back to their original shape.

3 Heat a wok, add 2 T. oil and heat. Fry the pouches until golden brown on both sides. Remove and cut into serving pieces. Serve.

1

2

芹菜豆包絲 · Stir-fried Celery and Tofu Pouches

油炸豆包 100公克	薑片 3片		
芹菜 55公克	**1**┌ 水 3大匙		
胡蘿蔔絲 30公克	├ 鹽 .... ½小匙		
香菇 10公克	└ 味精 .... ¼小匙		

1 芹菜去葉洗淨切4公分段；香菇泡軟洗淨去蒂切絲；
  油炸豆包（見39頁）切絲備用。
2 鍋熱入油2大匙燒熱，入香菇、薑片爆香，續入胡蘿
  蔔絲炒勻，再入**1**料及豆包、芹菜拌炒均勻即可。

3¹/₂oz.(100 g) .... fried
bean curd pouches
2 oz.(55 g) .... Chinese
celery
1 oz.(30 g)   shredded
carrots

¹/₃oz.(10 g) .... dried
black mushrooms
3 slices   ginger root
1┌ 3 T. .... water
　└ ¹/₂ t. .... salt

1 Discard the celery leaves, wash and cut stalks
  into 4 cm (1¹/₂") sections. Soak dried black
  mushrooms in warm water until soft, remove
  the stems and shred. Shred fried bean curd
  pouches (ref. P. 39).
2 Heat a wok, add 2 T. oil and heat. Stir-fry
  black mushrooms and sliced ginger root until
  fragrant. Add carrots and mix well. Add **1**,
  fried bean curd pouches and celery. Stir-fry until
  well-mixed. Serve.

三杯豆腐 · Basil Tofu

豆腐 450公克
九層塔（圖一）.. 50公克
麻油 4大匙
1 蒜頭、薑片 各20公克

2
水 1杯
酒 .... ¼杯
醬油 2大匙
糖 1小匙
味精 .... ¼小匙

1 lb.(450 g) .... tofu
1³/₄oz.(50 g) ...... basil
(illus.1)
4 T. .... sesame oil

2
1 C. .... water
¼ C. cooking wine
2 T. .... soy sauce
1 t. .... sugar

1
²/₃oz.(20 g)each:
garlic cloves,
ginger root slices

1 豆腐洗淨切2×2公分片狀，九層塔去老梗洗淨備用。

2 鍋熱入麻油燒熱，入**1**料炒至金黃色後撈起備用，鍋續入豆腐煎至金黃色，再入**1**、**2**料煮至湯汁收乾，最後入九層塔拌勻即可。

1 Rinse tofu and cut into 2×2 cm (1"×1") slices. Trim tough stalks off basil, use only the tender tips and leaves, wash.

2 Heat a wok, add sesame oil and heat. Stir-fry **1** until golden; remove **1** for later use. Add tofu and fry until golden. Add **1** and **2**, cook until the sauce is completely absorbed by tofu. Mix in basil and serve.

1

彭家豆腐 · Pong's Tofu Special

豆腐 400公克		高湯 1杯
蒜苗 1枝	**1**	蠔油、醬油　各1大匙
紅辣椒 1條		糖 1小匙
豆豉 1大匙		味精 1/8小匙
	2	水 1/2大匙
		太白粉 1/2小匙

1 豆腐切0.5公分厚之片狀，蒜苗洗淨切斜片，紅辣椒去籽切斜片備用。

2 鍋熱入油3大匙燒熱，入豆腐煎至兩面呈金黃色取出，續入豆豉炒香，再入豆腐及**1**料煮至湯汁快收乾，最後入蒜苗、辣椒拌勻並以**2**料勾芡即可。

14 oz.(400 g)...... tofu		1 C. .... stock
1 stalk .... fresh garlic	**1**	1 T. each: oyster
1 ..... red chili pepper		sauce, soy sauce
1 T. fermented black		1 t. .... sugar
beans	**2**	1/2 T. .... water
		1/2 t. ... cornstarch

1 Cut tofu into 0.5 cm (1/4") thick slices. Wash fresh garlic and cut into diagonal slices. Remove the seeds and slice the red chili pepper.

2 Heat a wok, add 3 T. oil and heat. Fry tofu slices to golden on both sides; remove. In the remaining oil, stir-fry fermented black beans until fragrant. Add tofu slices and **1**, cook until the sauce is nearly evaporated. Mix in fresh garlic and red chili pepper. Thicken with **2** and serve.

腐皮海帶 · Stir-fried Seaweed Knots

海帶結（圖一）	130公克	
油炸豆包	100公克	
胡蘿蔔	75公克	
蒜苗	28公克	
薑片	4片	

1
- 水 2大匙
- 醬油 1¹/₂大匙
- 酒、麻油 各2小匙
- 鹽、味精 ..... 各¹/₈小匙

4¹/₂oz.(130 g) .... sea
-weed knots (illus.1)
3¹/₂oz.(100 g) .... fried
bean curd pouches
2²/₃oz.(75 g) .. carrots
1 oz.(28 g).........fresh
garlic
4 slices ... ginger root

1
- 2 T. .... water
- 1¹/₂ T. .. soy sauce
- 2 t. each: cooking
  wine, sesame oil
- ¹/₈ t. .... salt

1 胡蘿蔔洗淨去皮切細絲；油炸豆包（見39頁）切絲；
  蒜苗洗淨切絲備用。

2 鍋熱入油1大匙燒熱，入薑片爆香，續入海帶結略炒，
  再入油炸豆包、胡蘿蔔及 **1** 料炒至湯汁略乾，最後入
  蒜苗拌勻即可。

1 Wash carrots, pare then shred. Shred fried
  bean curd pouches (ref. P. 39). Wash fresh
  garlic and shred.

2 Heat a wok, add 1 T. oil and heat. Stir-fry
  ginger root slices until fragrant. Add seaweed
  knots and fry slightly. Add shredded fried bean
  curd pouches, shredded carrots, and **1**; stir-fry
  until the sauce is nearly evaporated. Mix in
  shredded fresh garlic. Serve.

1

百頁蓮子 · Lotus Seeds and Pai Yeh Tofu

百頁豆腐（圖一）200公克
小黃瓜 70公克
蓮子 60公克
麻油 1/8小匙

1
┌紅辣椒 1條
└蒜片 1小匙

2
┌水 1/2杯
├蠔油 1小匙
└鹽 1/8小匙

7 oz.(200 g)... pai yeh tofu (illus.1)
2 1/2 oz.(70 g) gherkin cucumbers
2 oz.(60 g) lotus seeds
1/8 t. .... sesame oil

1
┌1 .... red chili pepper
└1 t. ... garlic clove slices

2
┌1/2 C. .... water
├1 t. ... oyster sauce
└1/8 t. .... salt

1 蓮子去心（圖二）加水1杯入鍋蒸軟，百頁豆腐、小黃瓜切片，紅辣椒去籽切片備用。

2 鍋熱入油2大匙燒熱，入 **1** 料爆香，續入百頁豆腐及 **2** 料煮至湯汁快收乾（約5分鐘），再入小黃瓜及蓮子拌勻，起鍋前撒上麻油即可。

■ 百頁豆腐可用普通豆腐代替。

1 Remove the green pits in the lotus seeds (illus.2), add 1 C. water and steam until tender. Remove the seeds from the red chili pepper. Cut pai yeh tofu, gherkin cucumbers and chili pepper into slices.

2 Heat a wok, add 2 T. oil and heat ; stir-fry **1** until fragrant. Add pai yeh tofu and **2**, cook until the sauce is nearly evaporated (about 5 minutes). Add gherkin cucumber slices and lotus seeds, mix well. Sprinkle on sesame oil and serve.

■ Pai yeh tofu can be replaced with tofu.

1

2

香韭豆干 · Warm Chive Flower Salad

五香豆干 300公克	┌ 水 3大匙	
韭菜花 150公克	酒 1大匙	
麻油 .... 少許	**1** 沙茶醬 2小匙	
	鹽 .... ½小匙	
	└ 味精 .... ⅛小匙	

1 韭菜花（圖一）洗淨切3公分長段，五香豆干切條狀備用。
2 鍋熱入油1大匙燒熱，入五香豆干及 **1** 料略炒，再入韭菜花拌炒至湯汁收乾，起鍋前入麻油拌勻即可。

■ 翡翠油豆腐：將五香豆干、韭菜花改成菠菜600公克、油豆腐皮125公克。其餘作法與香韭豆干同。

⅔ lb.(300 g) savory pressed bean curds	┌ 3 T. .... water	
⅓ lb.(150 g).... chives with flowering tips	1 T. cooking wine	
dash .... sesame oil	**1** 2 t. .... barbecue (sa-tsa)sauce	
	└ ½ t. .... salt	

1 Wash the chives with flowering tips (illus.1) and cut into 3 cm (1¼") sections. Cut the savory pressed bean curds into strips.
2 Heat a wok, add 1 T. oil and heat ; stir-fry savory pressed bean curd strips and **1** briefly. Add chives with flowering tips, mix and stir well; cook until the sauce evaporates completely. Mix in sesame oil and serve.

■ Spinach and Fried Tofu: Replace savory pressed bean curd and chives with flowering tips with 1⅓ lb. (600 g) spinach and 4⅓ oz. (125 g) of fried tofu skins. Seasoning and cooking methods are the same as above.

1

醬爆豆片 · Stir-fried Bean Curd with Bean Sauce

五香豆干 160公克
素火腿 80公克
青椒 50公克
洋蔥 20公克

豆瓣醬 1小匙
1 ┌水 1/4杯
  └醬油、糖 各1小匙

5²/₃oz.(160 g) savory pressed bean curds
2³/₄oz.(80 g) .... vegetarian ham
1³/₄oz.(50 g) ..... green bell peppers

²/₃oz.(20 g) ..... onions
1 t. .... bean paste
1 ┌ ¹/₄ C. .... water
  │ 1 t. each: sugar,
  └ soy sauce

1 豆干、素火腿（見38頁）、洋蔥洗淨切片，青椒洗淨去籽亦切片備用。

2 鍋熱入油1¹/₂大匙燒熱，入豆瓣醬炒香，續入洋蔥、素火腿、豆干拌炒數下，再入 **1** 料用小火煮3～4分鐘，最後拌入青椒即可。

1 Wash and slice savory pressed bean curd, vegetarian ham (ref. P. 38), and onions. Wash green bell pepper, discard the seeds and slice.

2 Heat a wok, add 1¹/₂ T. oil and heat ; stir-fry bean paste until fragrant. Add onions, vegetarian ham, and savory pressed bean curds; stir-fry and mix well. Add **1** and simmer over low heat for 3 or 4 minutes. Mix in green bell peppers and serve.

紅燒凍豆腐 · Soy Braised Frozen Tofu

凍豆腐 400公克
蒜苗 28公克
辣豆瓣醬 1小匙

1
┌ 蔥末 2大匙
└ 蒜末、薑末　各1小匙

2
┌ 水 1杯
│ 醬油 1½小匙
│ 醋 .... ½小匙
│ 糖、鹽 .... 各¼小匙
└ 味精 .... ⅛小匙

3
┌ 水 1大匙
└ 太白粉 1小匙

14 oz.(400 g) frozen tofu

1 oz.(28 g)fresh garlic

1 t. .. chili bean paste

1
┌ **2 T. .... minced green onions**
│ **1 t. each:minced garlic cloves ,**
└ **minced ginger root**

2
┌ **1 C. .... water**
│ **1½ t. .... soy sauce**
│ **½ t. .... vinegar**
│ **¼ t. each: sugar, salt**

3
┌ **1 T. .... water**
└ **1 t. ... cornstarch**

1 凍豆腐切成1×2公分塊狀，蒜苗洗淨斜切絲（圖一）備用。

2 鍋熱入油2大匙燒熱，入 **1** 料爆香，續入辣豆瓣醬炒香，隨即入凍豆腐及 **2** 料，改小火燜煮10分鐘，再以 **3** 料勾芡，起鍋前撒上蒜苗絲即可。

1 Cut tofu into 1 × 2 cm (½"×1") pieces. Wash fresh garlic and cut into diagonal shreds (illus.1).

2 Heat a wok, add 2 T. oil and heat. Stir-fry **1** until fragrant. Add chili bean paste and stir-fry until fragrant. Add tofu pieces and **2**, simmer over low heat for 10 minutes. Thicken with **3** . Sprinkle on shredded fresh garlic and serve.

1

紅糟雙味 · Crimson Bamboo shoots

筍（淨重）........ 170公克
麵輪（圖一）...... 75公克
紅糟（圖二）......... 1大匙

1┌水 .... 1 杯
　└糖、醬油 各1小匙

**6 oz.(170 g) bamboo shoots (net weight)
2 $\frac{2}{3}$oz.(75 g) .... wheat gluten wheels(illus.1)
1 T. ... red fermented wine rice (illus.2)**

1┌1 C. .... water
　│1 t. each: sugar,
　└soy sauce

1 麵輪泡水至軟，擠乾水份備用。
2 筍煮熟切滾刀塊。
3 鍋熱入油3大匙燒熱，入紅糟炒香，續入麵輪拌炒數下，再入筍及**1**料煮開後，改小火煮20分鐘至湯汁收乾即可。

1 Soak wheat gluten wheels in water until soft, Squeeze the water off.
2 Boil bamboo shoots until done, then cut into diagonal pieces.
3 Heat a wok, add 3 T. oil and heat. Stir-fry red fermented wine rice until fragrant. Add wheat gluten wheels and mix evenly. Add bamboo shoots and **1**, bring to a boil. Turn the heat to low and simmer for 20 minutes or until the sauce completely is evaporated. Serve.

1

2

55

薑絲麵腸 · Ginger Flavored Sausages

麵腸 300公克

薑絲 15公克

┌ 水 3大匙

1├ 醬油 1½大匙

└ 糖 1¼小匙

10½oz.(300 g) wheat gluten sausages

½oz.(15 g) shredded ginger root

┌ 3 T. .... water

1├ 1½ T. ... soy sauce

└ 1¼ t. .... sugar

1 麵腸對切後切片備用。

2 鍋熱入油2大匙燒熱，入薑絲爆香，續入麵腸用小火炒至呈金黃色（約2~3分鐘），再入**1**料煮至湯汁收乾即可。

1 Cut wheat gluten sausages in half lengthwise, then slice.

2 Heat a wok, add 2 T. oil and heat. Stir-fry shredded ginger root until fragrant. Add sausage slices and fry over low heat until golden (about 2 to 3 minutes). Add **1** and cook until the sauce is completely evaporated. Serve.

味噌麵腸 · Miso Flavored Sausages

麵腸 300公克	┌ 冷開水 3大匙
味噌 100公克	**1** │ 糖 2大匙
蔥末 2大匙	└ 熟白芝麻 1大匙

10¹/₂oz.(300 g) **wheat gluten sausages**
3¹/₂oz.(100 g) ... **miso**
2 T. .... **minced green onions**

┌ **3 T. .... cold water**
1 │ **2 T. .... sugar**
│ **1 T. roasted white**
└ **sesame seeds**

1 麵腸切小塊（圖一）入開水中煮5分鐘後，撈起瀝乾待涼置盤。
2 **1**料入果汁機打至芝麻變碎，與味噌拌勻淋在麵腸上，再撒上蔥末即可。

1 Cut the wheat gluten sausages into small serving pieces (illus.1), boil in boiling water for 5 minutes. Drain and leave to cool. Arrange them on a plate.
2 Beat **1** in a juicer until sesame seeds are finely crushed; mix with miso and pour over the wheat gluten sausages. Sprinkle on minced green onions and serve.

1

番茄烘蛋 • Tomato Egg Cake

1	番茄 .... 150公克 洋蔥 .... 90公克 洋菇 40公克	蛋 .... 6個 **2** 鹽 .... ¹/₂小匙 胡椒粉 .... ¹/₄小匙		

1 ⎧ ¹/₃ lb.(150 g) .... tomatoes 3¹/₄oz.(90 g)onions 1²/₃oz.(40 g) .... mushrooms

6 .... eggs
2 ⎧ ¹/₂ t. .... salt ¹/₄ t. .... pepper

1 番茄洗淨後，底部用刀劃成十字，入開水中川燙後
（約2分鐘）撈起，置冷水中去皮；洋菇亦入開水中
川燙，撈起漂涼，瀝乾備用。

2 **1**料均切小丁，鍋熱入油2小匙燒熱，入洋蔥炒至呈
透明狀，再入番茄及洋菇拌炒均勻。

3 蛋打散，入**2**料及炒熟之**1**料拌勻備用。

4 鍋熱入油3大匙燒熱，入蛋液蓋鍋蓋以小火烘至半凝
固狀後，翻面續烘20秒即可。

1 Wash the tomatoes, score a cross on the bottoms; scald in boiling water (about 2 minutes). Remove and drop into cold water to remove the skins. Scald the mushrooms, rinse under cold water and pat dry.

2 Dice all ingredients in **1** . Heat a wok, add 2 t. oil and heat; stir-fry diced onions until transparent. Add diced tomatoes and diced mushrooms, stir-fry and mix well.

3 Beat the eggs, season with **2** and mix in cooked **1** .

4 Heat a wok, add 3 T. oil and heat; pour in the egg mixture. Cover with a lid and pot bake over low heat until half set. Turn the egg cake and bake the other side for 20 seconds. Serve.

瓠瓜烘蛋 · Gourd Egg Cake

瓠瓜（圖一）.... 280公克		水 3大匙
蛋 3個		酒 1小匙
蒜末 1小匙	**1**	鹽 1/2小匙
		味精 1/4小匙

12$\frac{1}{3}$oz.(280 g) .... gourd (illus.1)

3 ....eggs

1 t. ..... minced garlic cloves

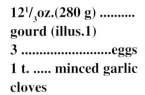

1	3 T. .... water
	1 t. .. cooking wine
	1/2 t . ... salt

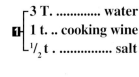

1　瓠瓜去皮切小丁泡水，蛋打散備用。

2　鍋熱入油1大匙燒熱，入蒜末爆香，續入瓠瓜拌炒數下，再入 **1** 料煮至瓠瓜變軟（約5分鐘），盛起入蛋液中攪拌均勻備用。

3　鍋熱入油3大匙燒熱，入蛋液並蓋上鍋蓋改小火烘7分鐘後，盛盤切12等份即可。

1　Pare the gourd, dice and soak in water. Beat the eggs.

2　Heat a wok, add 1 T. oil and heat; stir-fry minced garlic cloves until fragrant. Add drained, diced gourd and stir-fry slightly. Season with **1** and cook until soft (about 5 minutes). Pour the mixture into beaten eggs and mix well.

3　Heat a wok, add 3 T. oil and heat, pour in the egg mixture. Cover with a lid and pot bake over low heat for 7 minutes. Remove to a plate and slice into 12 equal pieces. Serve.

1

素茶碗蒸 • Vegetarian Chawamushi

蛋 5個	┌ 醬油 1大匙	
豆漿 2¹/₂杯	**1**├ 鹽 .... ¹/₂小匙	
玉米醬 .... ¹/₂杯	└ 味精 .... ¹/₄小匙	
蔥末 2大匙		

1 蛋打散加豆漿、玉米醬及**1**料拌勻，入蒸鍋以小火蒸
　15分鐘，取出撒上蔥末即可。

5 .... **eggs**
2¹/₂ **C.** .... **soy bean milk**
¹/₂ **C. .. creamed corn**

2 T. .... **minced green onions**

1┌ 1 T. ...... **soy sauce**
　└ ¹/₂ t. .... **salt**

1　Beat the eggs, add soy bean milk, creamed
　corn, and**1** ; mix well. Steam over low heat
　for 15 minutes. Remove and sprinkle on
　minced green onions. Serve.

60

翡翠蒸蛋 • Steamed Green Jade Eggs

菠菜 110公克	糖 .... ½小匙		
蘿蔔乾（圖一） 40公克	**1**┌鹽 .... ¾小匙		
蛋 4個	└酒 .... ½小匙		

$3^3/_4$oz.(110 g) spinach
$1^1/_3$oz.(40 g) ....
salt-preserved daikon
(illus.1)
1┌ ¾ t. .... salt
└ ½ t. cooking wine

½ t. .... sugar

4 .... eggs

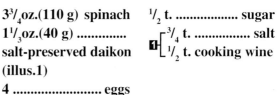

1 蘿蔔乾洗淨切碎；鍋熱入油1小匙燒熱，入蘿蔔乾炒香，再加糖調味備用。

2 菠菜洗淨瀝乾切小段，加水1½杯入果汁機打成汁備用。

3 蛋打散，入**1**料、菠菜汁及⅔的蘿蔔乾拌勻，置蒸碗內，入鍋以小火蒸15分鐘，再撒上剩餘的蘿蔔乾，續蒸5～8分鐘即可。

1 Wash and mince salt-preserved daikon. Heat a wok, add 1 t. oil and heat. Stir-fry salt-preserved daikon until fragrant, season with sugar.

2 Wash spinach and pat dry, cut into short sections. Add $1^1/_2$ C. water and puree to spinach juice in a juicer.

3 Beat the eggs, add **1**, $^2/_3$ of salt-preserved daikon and spinach juice; mix well. Pour the egg mixture into a large bowl. Steam over low heat for 15 minutes. Sprinkle on the remaining $^1/_3$ salt-preserved daikon and continue steaming for another 5 to 8 minutes. Serve.

1

素和菜戴帽 · Egg-capped Vegetables

菠菜 170公克	
豆芽菜 150公克	
韭黃（圖一）.... 100公克	
豆干 65公克	
粉絲1把 28公克	
蛋 2個	

1
水 .... ¹/₄杯
鹽、麻油........各¹/₂小匙
美極鮮味露 ... ¹/₄小匙
味精、胡椒粉 ....
.... 各¹/₈小匙

6 oz.(170 g)　spinach
¹/₃ lb.(150 g)..............
bean sprouts
3¹/₂oz.(100 g)　yellow
chives (illus.1)
2¹/₄oz.(65 g)　pressed
bean curds
2 .... eggs

1 oz.(28 g) .... bean
threads

1
¹/₄ C. .... water
¹/₂ t. each: sesame
oil, salt
¹/₄ t. Maggie sauce
¹/₈ t. .... pepper

1 菠菜、韭黃洗淨後切4公分段，粉絲（見23頁）加水泡5分鐘後，瀝乾切5公分段；豆干洗淨切絲。

2 蛋打散加鹽¹/₈小匙拌勻，鍋熱取紗布沾油塗在鍋子上，入蛋液煎成一張蛋皮備用。

3 鍋熱入油2大匙燒熱，入豆干炒軟，續入韭黃拌炒數下，再入粉絲、豆芽菜及**1**料拌炒約1分鐘，最後入菠菜炒軟，隨即起鍋排盤再蓋上蛋皮即可。

1 Wash spinach and yellow chives, cut both into 4 cm (1¹/₂ ") sections. Soak bean threads (ref. P. 23) in water for 5 minutes, drain and cut into 5 cm (2") sections. Wash pressed bean curds and shred.

2 Beat the eggs and mix in ¹/₈ t. salt. Heat a pan and brush on a thin film of oil. Pour in beaten eggs and make one egg crepe.

3 Heat a wok, add 2 T. oil and heat. Stir-fry pressed bean curds until tender. Add yellow chives and fry slightly. Add bean threads, bean sprouts, and **1**, stir-fry for one minute. Add spinach and stir-fry until tender. Remove the vegetables to a plate and top with the egg crepe. Serve.

1

皮蛋莧菜 · Ra-hden and Preserved Egg

莧菜 400公克	麻油 1小匙	**12 oz.(400 g) .... ra-hden**	**1 T. ..... cooking wine**
蒜頭 10公克	水 .... ¼杯	**⅓oz.(10 g) ...... garlic cloves**	**1 t. .... sesame oil**
皮蛋 1個	**❶** 鹽、味精、胡椒粉 ...	**1 .... preserved egg**	**❶** ¼ C. .... water
酒 1大匙	.... 各¼小匙		¼ t. each: pepper, salt

1 莧菜洗淨去根（圖一）及老纖維後，洗淨切3公分段，皮蛋去殼（圖二）切小丁，蒜頭略拍備用。

2 鍋熱入油3大匙燒熱，入蒜頭爆香至金黃色，續入莧菜、酒及❶料炒軟，改小火燜煮3分鐘，起鍋前入皮蛋、麻油拌勻即可。

1 Wash and discard the tough ends of the ra-hden (illus.1), cut into 3 cm (1") long sections. Peel the shell (illus.2) and dice the preserved egg. Peel the skins off the garlic cloves and crush with the back of a knife.

2 Heat a wok, add 3 T. oil and heat. Stir-fry garlic cloves until golden and fragrant. Add ra-hden, cooking wine, and season with **❶**; stir-fry until tender. Turn the heat low and simmer for 3 more minutes. Mix in preserved egg and sesame oil. Serve.

1

2

桂花炒魚翅 · Stir-fried Shark Fins

素魚翅（圖一） 115公克	香菇 6朵
┌筍絲 75公克	蛋 4個
1├荸薺 42公克	麻油 3大匙
└胡蘿蔔絲 28公克	**2** 鹽、胡椒粉 各¹/₄小匙
	3┌鹽、味精、糖 ....
	└ .... 各¹/₄小匙

¹/₄ **lb. (115 g) ....**	**6 .... dried black**
vegetarian shark	**mushrooms**
fins (illus.1)	**4 .... eggs**
┌ **2²/₃ oz.(75 g) ....**	**3 T. .... sesame oil**
shredded bamboo	**2**┌ ¹/₄ **t. each:pepper,**
shoots	└ **salt**
1├ **1¹/₂ oz.(42 g) ....**	**3**┌ ¹/₄ **t. each: sugar,**
water chestnuts	└ **salt**
1 oz.(28 g)	
└ **shredded carrots**	

1 素魚翅入開水中煮5分鐘後，取出瀝乾水份；香菇泡軟洗淨去蒂切絲，荸薺洗淨去皮拍碎；蛋打散備用。

2 鍋熱入麻油3大匙燒熱，入香菇絲炒香，續入**1**料炒勻並以**2**料調味後盛起，入蛋液中拌勻。

3 鍋熱入油3大匙燒熱，入蛋液炒至完全凝固，再入素魚翅及**3**料拌炒均勻即可。

1 Boil vegetarian shark fins in boiling water for 5 minutes, drain. Soak dried black mushrooms in warm water, wash and remove the stems; shred. Wash water chestnuts, pare and crush with the back of a knife. Beat the eggs.

2 Heat a wok, add 3 T. sesame oil and heat. Stir-fry shredded black mushrooms until fragrant. Add **1**, stir-fry and mix well. Season with **2**. Remove from the wok. Mix the vegetable mixture into the beaten eggs.

3 Heat a wok, add 3 T. oil and heat. Stir-fry the egg mixture until completely set. Add shark fins and **3**; stir-fry and mix well. Serve.

1

鐵板太陽蛋 · Sunny-side-up on Sizzling Plate

蛋 4個	┌ 水 4大匙
洋蔥 100公克	番茄醬 2大匙
奶油 1大匙	糖 1¹/₃大匙
	❶ 醬油 1大匙
	檸檬汁 1小匙
	太白粉、黑胡椒粉 ...
	└ .... 各¹/₂小匙

4 .... eggs	┌ 4 T. .... water
3¹/₂oz.(100 g) ...onion	2 T. .... ketchup
1 T. .... butter	1¹/₃ T. .... sugar
	❶ 1 T. ...... soy sauce
	1 t. ... lemon juice
	¹/₂ t. each: black
	pepper powder,
	└ cornstarch

1 洋蔥洗淨切絲；鐵板燒熱，入奶油加熱至融化，續入洋蔥絲，改小火使鐵板維持熱度。

2 另鍋熱入油2大匙燒熱，蛋去殼入鍋，以小火煎至蛋白凝固，盛起置於洋蔥上，依序將蛋煎完。

3 ❶料入鍋以小火煮至濃稠，淋於蛋上即可。

1 Pare and wash the onion; shred. Heat a plate, add butter and heat until butter melts. Add shredded onions. Turn the heat low, but enough to keep the plate hot.

2 Heat a wok, add 2 T. oil and heat. Fry an egg over low heat until the egg white sets. Remove the egg and put on top of the onions. Repeat with the remaining three eggs.

3 Boil ❶ in a small pot over low heat until thickened. Pour the sauce over the eggs. Serve on the hot plate.

什錦砂鍋 · Assorted Vegetable Casserole

大白菜	225公克	薑片	3片
凍豆腐	150公克	┌高湯	5杯
蒟蒻	85公克	│酒	1大匙
筍（淨重）	55公克	❶蠔油	2小匙
胡蘿蔔	14公克	│鹽	1小匙
香菇	6朵	└胡椒粉	¼小匙
蔥段	6段		

8 oz.(225 g).... nappa cabbage
5$\frac{1}{3}$oz. (150 g) frozen tofu
3 oz.(85 g) shirataki
2 oz.(55 g)... bamboo shoots (net weight)
$\frac{1}{2}$oz.(14 g) .... carrots
6 .... dried black mushrooms

6 sections .... green onion
3 slices ... ginger root
┌ 5 C. .... stock
│ 1 T. cooking wine
❶ 2 t. ... oyster sauce
│ 1 t. .... salt
└ ¼ t. .... pepper

1 凍豆腐切塊，香菇泡軟洗淨去蒂切塊，胡蘿蔔去皮切片，蒟蒻（圖一）切花，筍入鍋煮熟切塊，大白菜洗淨切大塊備用。

2 砂鍋熱入油2大匙燒熱，入蔥、薑、香菇爆香，續入大白菜炒軟，隨即入❶料煮開，再入胡蘿蔔、凍豆腐、筍塊、蒟蒻煮開後改小火煮15分鐘即可。

■ 凍豆腐之製作─將豆腐放入冷凍庫中結冰後，取出再退冰即為凍豆腐。

1 Cut the frozen tofu into serving squares. Soak the dried black mushrooms in warm water until soft, remove the stems and cut into serving pieces. Pare off the skin and slice the carrot. Score the surface of shirataki (illus.1) and cut into serving pieces. Boil bamboo shoots in the water until cooked and cut into serving pieces. Wash nappa cabbage and cut into large serving picces.

2 Heat a casserole, add 2 T. oil and heat. Stir-fry green onions, ginger root and black mushrooms until fragrant. Add nappa cabbage and stir-fry until tender. Pour in ❶ and bring to a boil. Add carrots, frozen tofu, bamboo shoots, and shirataki and bring to a boil again. Turn heat to low and simmer for 15 minutes. Serve.

■Frozen tofu: Place tofu in freezer until frozen. Remove from freezer and defrost.

1

六人份 SERVES 6

菜肉餛飩 · Wonton Soup Classic

小白菜 225公克	┌ 太白粉 1¹/₂大匙
餛飩皮 140公克	**1** │ 麻油、水 各1大匙
榨菜 85公克	└
素火腿（見38頁）55公克	┌ 麻油 2小匙
蛋 1個	**2** │ 醬油 1小匙
紫菜 .... ²/₃張	│ 鹽 .... ¹/₂小匙
高湯 6杯	└ 味精 .... ¹/₈小匙

1 小白菜洗淨，入開水中川燙至軟，撈起漂涼，擠乾水份並剁碎；榨菜洗淨取²/₃量切末，另¹/₃切絲，素火腿切末備用。

2 小白菜、榨菜末及素火腿加 **1** 料拌勻，取¹/₂小匙置於餛飩皮中間，對角摺成三角形（圖一），再向上折半（圖二），最後兩角對疊（圖三）並沾水黏緊即為餛飩。

3 鍋熱取紗布沾油塗在鍋子上，入打散之蛋液煎成蛋皮，盛起待涼切絲；紫菜對半剪開，再剪成1公分寬之絲狀備用。

4 高湯煮開，入餛飩及榨菜絲煮開，再入 **2** 料調味後熄火，置大碗中上撒蛋皮絲及紫菜絲即可。

8 oz.(225 g) Chinese cabbage	**²/₃ sheet .... seaweed (nori)**
5 oz.(140 g) wonton wrappers	**6 C. .... stock**
3 oz.(85 g) ..... pickled mustard head	┌ **1¹/₂ T. cornstarch**
	1 │ **1 T. each:**
2 oz.(55 g) vegetarian ham (ref. P. 38)	└ **sesame oil, water**
	┌ **2 t. ...... sesame oil**
1 .... egg	**2** │ **1 t. .... soy sauce**
	└ **¹/₂ t. .... salt**

1 Wash Chinese cabbage and parboil in boiling water until tender; drain and squeeze off excess water; mince. Wash pickled mustard head, minced ²/₃, and shred the other ¹/₃. Mince vegetarian ham.

2 Mix minced Chinese cabbage, minced pickled mustard head, minced vegetarian ham, and **1** for the wonton filling. Place ¹/₂ t. filling in the center of one wonton wrapper, fold diagonally to form a triangle (illus.1), then fold again to half (illus.2). Dip a drop of water on one corner and press the other corner onto that corner (illus.3).

3 Heat a pan, brush on a thin film of oil, pour in beaten egg to make egg crepe. Remove and shred when cool. Snip dried seaweed to half, then snip into 1 cm (¹/₂") wide shreds.

4 Bring the stock to a boil, add wontons and shredded pickled mustard head; bring to a boil and season with **2**. Pour the wonton soup into a large bowl or individual bowls. Sprinkle on shredded egg crepe and shredded dried seaweed. Serve.

1

2

3

蔬菜羹 · Mixed Vegetable Porridge

大白菜 450公克
金針菇 100公克
濕木耳 56公克
胡蘿蔔 28公克
香菇 14公克
蔥段 6段
薑絲、香菜末 各1大匙

1
高湯 5杯
醬油、酒 各1大匙
蠔油、鹽、糖各1小匙
胡椒粉 1/4小匙

2
水 3大匙
太白粉 2大匙

3
烏醋、麻油　各1大匙
沙茶醬 2小匙

1 lb. (450 g) ... nappa cabbage
3¹/₂oz.(100 g) golden mushrooms (enoki)
2 oz.(56 g) ..... soaked wood ears
1 oz.(28 g) ..... carrots
¹/₂oz.(14 g) .... dried black mushrooms
6 section .... green onions
1 T. each: shredded ginger root, minced coriander

1
5 C. .... stock
1 T. each:soy sauce, cooking wine
1 t. each: oyster sauce, sugar, salt
¹/₄ t. .... pepper

2
3 T. .... water
2 T. ... cornstarch

3
1 T. each: black vinegar, sesame oil
2 t. .... barbecue (sa-tsa)sauce

1 香菇泡軟洗淨去蒂切絲，大白菜洗淨切塊，金針菇
　（見22頁）去頭洗淨，胡蘿蔔洗淨切片，木耳洗淨去
　蒂切絲備用。

2 鍋熱入油3大匙燒熱，入香菇絲、蔥段、薑絲爆香，
　續入大白菜炒軟，隨即入**1**料煮開，再入金針菇、木
　耳、胡蘿蔔，改小火煮20分鐘，以**2**料勾芡，最後入
　3料拌勻並撒上香菜末即可。

1 Soak dried black mushrooms in warm water until soft, wash and remove the stems; shred. Wash nappa cabbage and cut into serving pieces. Trim off the ends of golden mushrooms (ref. P. 22) and wash. Wash carrots and slice. Wash wood ears and remove the stems; shred.

2 Heat a wok, add 3 T. oil and heat. Stir-fry shredded black mushrooms, green onion sections, and shredded ginger root until fragrant. Add nappa cabbage and stir-fry until tender. Pour in **1** and bring to a boil. Add golden mushrooms , wood ears and carrot slices, simmer over low heat for 20 minutes. Thicken with **2** , and mix in**3** . Sprinkle on minced coriander and serve.

蔬菜濃湯 · Minestrone

紅番茄	300公克	麵粉	½杯
馬鈴薯	225公克	┌高湯	5½杯
玉米粒	170公克	│奶水	½杯
洋蔥	115公克	**1**┤鹽	1小匙
奶油	60公克	│胡椒粉	½小匙
菠菜葉	50公克	└月桂葉	1片

10½ oz.(300 g) red tomatoes		½ C.	flour
8 oz.(225 g) potatoes		┌5½ C.	stock
6 oz.(170 g) corn		│½ C.	evaporated milk
¼ lb.(115 g) onions		**1**┤1 t.	salt
2 oz.(60 g) butter		│½ t.	pepper
1¾ oz.(50 g) spinach leaves		└1	bay leaves

1 馬鈴薯去皮切小丁，入鍋煮軟，撈起瀝乾備用。番茄底部劃十字入開水中川燙，隨即取出漂涼去皮及籽，再切小丁；洋蔥切小丁，菠菜葉洗淨後切絲備用。

2 鍋熱入奶油加熱至融化，入洋蔥炒軟，續入麵粉炒香，隨即入**1**料煮開，再入馬鈴薯、玉米粒、番茄丁煮10分鐘，最後入菠菜葉拌勻即可。

1 Pare the potatoes and dice, boil until tender; drain. Score a cross at the bottom of each tomato, scald in boiling water; rinse under cold water to cool. Remove the tomato skins and seeds, dice. Dice onions. Wash spinach leaves and shred.

2 Heat a skillet, add butter and heat until melted, stir-fry diced onion until tender. Add flour to fry until fragrant. Pour in **1** and bring to a boil. Add potatoes, corn, and tomatoes, boil for 10 minutes. Mix in shredded spinach and serve.

白玉羹 • White Jade Porridge

嫩豆腐 2塊	┌鹽 1小匙
雪裡紅 110公克	**1**├糖、胡椒粉 各½小匙
熟筍 70公克	└味精 .... ¼小匙
香菇 15公克	┌水 2大匙
高湯 5杯	**2**└太白粉 1⅓大匙
麻油 2大匙	

1 豆腐洗淨切絲，香菇泡軟洗淨去蒂與熟筍均切細絲備用。

2 鍋熱入麻油2大匙燒熱，入香菇爆香，再入雪裡紅拌炒數下，起鍋備用。

3 高湯煮開，入豆腐、筍絲及**1**料煮5分鐘，續入雪裡紅、香菇煮開，再以**2**料勾芡即可。

2 cakes .... soft tofu	5 C. .... stock
3¾oz.(110 g) salted mustard greens	2 T. .... sesame oil
2½oz.(70 g) .... boiled bamboo shoots	**1**┌ 1 t. .... salt └ ½ t. each: sugar, pepper
½oz.(15 g)dried black mushrooms	**2**┌ 2 T. .... water └ 1⅓ T. cornstarch

1 Rinse tofu cakes and shred. Soak dried black mushrooms in warm water until soft, remove the stems and shred. Shred the bamboo shoots.

2 Heat a wok, add 2 T. sesame oil and heat. Stir-fry black mushrooms until fragrant. Add salted mustard greens, mix evenly. Remove.

3 Bring the stock to a boil, add tofu, bamboo shoots, and **1**, boil for 5 minutes. Add salted mustard and black mushrooms, bring to a boil again. Thicken with **2**. Serve.

73

福祿壽湯 · Fortune Soup

油炸豆包、金針菇 ....
.... 各60公克
蒜苗 40公克
香菇 8朵
蛋 2個
麻油 1小匙

1
┌ 美極鮮味露 1大匙
│ 鹽 .... $\frac{1}{2}$小匙
└ 胡椒粉 .... $\frac{1}{4}$小匙

2
┌ 水 1大匙
└ 太白粉 1小匙

2 oz.(60 g)each:fried
bean curd pouches ,
golden mushrooms
(enoki)
$1\frac{1}{3}$oz.(40 g) ......fresh
garlic
8 .... dried black
mushrooms

2 .... eggs
1 t. .... sesame oil

1
┌ 1 T. Maggie sauce
│ $\frac{1}{2}$ t. .... salt
└ $\frac{1}{4}$ t. .... pepper

2
┌ 1 T. .... water
└ 1 t. ..... cornstarch

1 香菇泡軟洗淨去蒂切絲；油炸豆包（見39頁）亦切
絲；蒜苗切細圈狀；蛋打勻備用。

2 鍋內入水5杯煮開，入香菇絲、金針菇（見22頁）及
油炸豆包煮5分鐘後，續入**1**料及蒜苗煮開，再以**2**
料勾芡，隨即入蛋液煮開，最後灑上麻油即可。

1 Soak black mushrooms in warm water, remove
the stems and shred. Shred fried bean curd
pouches (ref. P. 39). Cut fresh garlic into small
rings. Beat the eggs.

2 Bring 5 C. water to a boil, add shredded black
mushrooms, golden mushrooms (ref. P. 22)
and shredded fried bean curd pouches and boil
for 5 minutes. Add **1** and fresh garlic and bring
to a boil. Thicken with **2** . Pour in beaten eggs
and bring to a boil again. Sprinkle on sesame
oil and serve.

髮菜羹 · Black Moss Porridge

大白菜 225公克	┌烏醋 1大匙
筍絲 75公克	│蝦油 2小匙
胡蘿蔔絲 58公克	**1**│紹興酒、麻油、鹽、
香菇 14公克	│糖 各1小匙
髮菜（圖一）........ 7公克	└味精 1/4小匙
蔥段 6段	┌水 4大匙
高湯 5杯	**2**└太白粉 2大匙
香菜 .... 少許	

8 oz.(225 g)..... nappa cabbage
2²/₃oz.(75 g)shredded bamboo shoots
2 oz.(58 g) shredded carrots
¹/₂oz.(14 g) ...... dried black mushrooms
¹/₄oz.(7 g) .... dried black moss (illus.1)
6 sections green onion

5 C. .... stock
a dash of   coriander

1 ┌ 1 T. black vinegar
2 t. shrimp sauce
1 t. each:Chinese Shao-Shin wine, sesame oil, salt, sugar

2 ┌ 4 T. .... water
2 T. .... cornstarch

1 髮菜洗淨泡軟；香菇泡軟洗淨去蒂切絲；大白菜亦洗淨切絲備用。

2 鍋熱入油2大匙燒熱，入蔥段、香菇爆香，再入大白菜炒軟，續入高湯、筍絲、胡蘿蔔絲煮5分鐘後，入 **1** 料及髮菜煮開，最後以 **2** 料勾芡，起鍋前灑上香菜即可。

1 Wash dried black moss and soak in water until soft. Soak dried black mushrooms until soft, wash, discard the stems and shred. Wash the nappa cabbage and shred.

2 Heat a wok, add 2 T. oil and heat; stir-fry green onion sections and shredded black mushrooms until fragrant. Add shredded nappa cabbage and stir-fry until soft. Pour in stock, shredded bamboo shoots and shredded carrots; boil for 5 minutes.   Season with **1** and add hair seaweed. Bring to a boil and thicken with **2** . Sprinkle on coriander and serve.

1

香菇筍片湯 · Bamboo Soup

綠竹筍	450公克	高湯	6杯
芹菜末	50公克	**1**[鹽	1小匙
香菇	15公克	味精	¹/₄小匙

1 lb.(450 g) ...... green bamboo shoots	¹/₂oz.(15 g)dried black mushrooms
1³/₄oz.(50 g) minced Chinese celery	6 C. .... stock
	1 t. .... salt

1 綠竹筍去殼（圖一）及老纖維後切滾刀塊，香菇泡軟洗淨去蒂切片備用。

2 鍋熱入油2大匙燒熱，入香菇爆香，續入筍塊及高湯煮開後改小火煮30分鐘，再入**1**料調味，起鍋置湯碗再撒上芹菜末即可。

1 Peel the skins off the green bamboo shoots (illus.1) and trim off the tough fiber; cut into diagonal pieces. Soak the dried black mushrooms in warm water until soft, remove the stems and slice.

2 Heat a wok, add 2 T. oil and heat. Stir-fry black mushrooms until fragrant. Add green bamboo shoots and stock, bring to a boil. Turn the heat to low and simmer for 30 minutes. Season with salt. Sprinkle on minced Chinese celery and serve.

1

竹笙大補湯 · Bamboo Pith and Herb Soup

筍（淨重）........ 200公克
白果（見26頁）100公克
香菇 15公克
竹笙（圖一）...... 10公克
高湯 5杯

1　紅棗（見39頁）.........
　　　...................... 20公克
　　枸杞 5公克
　　參鬚、當歸 各3公克

2　酒 2大匙
　　鹽 1小匙
　　糖 1/2小匙
　　胡椒粉 1/8小匙

7 oz.(200 g) bamboo
shoots (net weight)
3¹/₂oz.(100 g) ....
ginkgo nuts (ref. P. 26)
¹/₂oz.(15 g) .... dried
black mushrooms
¹/₃oz.(10 g)   bamboo
pith fungus (illus.1)
5 C. .... stock

1　²/₃oz.(20 g) .... red
jujubes (ref. P. 39)
¹/₆oz.(5 g) lycium
berries
3 g each: fibrous
ginseng, tangkuei

2　2 T. cooking wine
1 t. .... salt
¹/₂ t. .... sugar
¹/₈ t. .... pepper

1　香菇泡軟洗淨去蒂，竹笙泡軟，筍洗淨，三者均切塊，**1**料稍沖洗，紅棗用刀劃數刀備用。

2　水3杯煮開，入竹笙及白果煮10分鐘，取出漂涼備用。

3　燉盅入高湯、筍塊、白果、香菇、竹笙及**1**料，入鍋蒸1小時後，以**2**料調味即可。

1　Soak dried black mushrooms and bamboo pith fungus in water until soft, remove the black mushroom stems; cut both into serving pieces. Wash bamboo shoots and cut into serving pieces. Rinse **1**, score the red jujubes.

2　Bring 3 C. water to a boil, add bamboo pith fungus and ginkgo nuts and cook for 10 minutes. Drain and rinse cool.

3　In a ceramic pot, add stock, bamboo shoots, ginkgo nuts, black mushrooms, bamboo pith fungus, and **1**. Steam in a steamer for one hour. Season with **2** and serve.

1

77

素魚翅羹 · Shark Fins Porridge

熟筍		170公克
素魚翅		150公克
香菜		20公克
香菇		6朵
蔥段		8段
薑片		5片
高湯		5杯

1 水、太白粉 各2大匙

2
- 蔥段 4段
- 薑片 3片
- 酒 2大匙

3
- 醬油、酒 各2大匙
- 烏醋、麻油 各2小匙
- 糖 1½小匙
- 鹽 .... ¼小匙
- 胡椒粉、味精 ....
  .... 各⅛小匙

6 oz.(170 g) ..... boiled bamboo shoots
⅓ lb.(150 g) .... vegetarian shark fins
⅔ oz.(20 g) coriander
6 .... dried black mushrooms
8 sections green onion
5 slices ... ginger root
5 C. .... stock

1 ⎡ 2 T. each: water, cornstarch

2
- 4 sections .... green onion
- 3 slices ginger root
- 2 T. cooking wine

3
- 2 T. each:soy sauce, cooking wine
- 2 t. each: black vinegar, sesame oil
- 1½ t. .... sugar
- ¼ t. .... salt
- ⅛ t. .... pepper

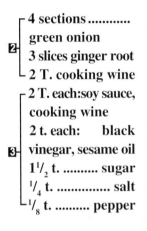

1 **2**料加水煮開,入素魚翅(見64頁)川燙後撈起;香菇泡軟洗淨去蒂切絲;筍切絲,香菜洗淨切末備用。

2 鍋熱入油2大匙燒熱,入蔥段、薑片及香菇爆香,續入魚翅、筍絲拌炒,再入高湯及**3**料煮開後,改小火煮10分鐘,最後以**1**料勾芡並撒上香菜末即可。

1 Bring water and **2** to a boil, parboil vegetarian shark fins (ref. P. 64) in the liquid; remove and drain. Soak dried black mushrooms in water until soft, remove the stems and shred. Shred the bamboo shoots. Wash coriander and mince.

2 Heat a wok, add 2 T. oil and heat. Stir-fry green onion sections, ginger root slices, and shredded dried black mushrooms until fragrant. Add shark fins and shredded bamboo shoots and fry. Add stock and **3** , bring to a boil. Turn the heat to low and simmer for 10 minutes. Thicken with **1** and sprinkle on minced coriander. Serve.

香菇素雞湯 · Mushroom and Herb Soup

素雞（圖一）.... 225公克	紅棗（見39頁）...... 12個	¹/₂ lb.(225 g)vegetarian chicken (illus.1)	12 .... red jujubes (ref . P. 39)
香菇 14公克	枸杞 2大匙	¹/₂ oz.(14 g) .... dried black mushrooms	2 T. ... lycium berries
蔥 10段	❶ ⌈高湯 5杯	10 sections .... green onion	❶ ⌈5 C. .... stock
薑片 4片	⌊鹽、味精 ..... 各¹/₂小匙	4 slices ... ginger root	⌊¹/₂ t. .... salt

1 香菇泡軟洗淨去蒂，切成4片；素雞切大塊。

2 鍋熱入油1大匙燒熱，入蔥段、薑片及香菇爆香，再入❶料煮開，取出置燉盅內，續入素雞、枸杞、紅棗後，蓋上蓋子入蒸鍋蒸20分鐘，取出撈去蔥段即可。

1 Soak dried black mushrooms in warm water until soft, discard the stems and cut into quarters. Cut the vegetarian chicken into large serving pieces.

2 Heat a wok, add 1 T. oil and heat ; stir-fry the green onion sections, ginger root slices, and dried black mushrooms until fragrant. Add ❶ and bring to a boil. Pour the soup into a ceramic steam pot, add vegetarian chicken, lycium berries and red jujubes; cover with a lid and steam for 20 minutes. Discard the green onion sections and serve.

1

清香南瓜盅 • Steamed Pumpkin Cup

南瓜（1個）.... 1500公克	高湯 3杯	
香菇 7朵	**2**⎡ 熟筍 75公克	
1⎡ 鹽 .... ⁵⁄₈小匙	⎢ 木耳 50公克	
⎢ 味精、胡椒粉	⎣ 金針 15公克	
⎣ .... 各¹⁄₈小匙		

$3^1/_4$ lb.(1500 g) .... pumpkin

7 .... dried black mushrooms

3 C. .... stock

1⎡ $^5/_8$ t. .... salt
⎣ $^1/_8$ t. .... pepper

2⎡ $2^2/_3$ oz.(75 g)boiled **bamboo shoots**
⎢ $1^3/_4$ oz.(50 g)**wood ears**
⎣ $^1/_2$ oz.(15 g) **dried lily buds**

1 南瓜外皮刷洗乾淨，於蒂下2公分處橫切開作為盅蓋，再修整盅口，並挖除南瓜內之籽備用。

2 香菇泡軟洗淨去蒂切絲，金針（見28頁）洗淨泡軟打結，熟筍、木耳分別洗淨切絲備用。

3 鍋熱入油¹⁄₂大匙燒熱，入香菇炒香，續入**2**料及高湯煮開，盛入南瓜盅內，蓋上盅蓋，入鍋以中火蒸至南瓜熟爛（約50分鐘），再以**1**料調味即可。

1 Brush the pumpkin skin clean, cut off the top (about 2 cm or 1" under the stem) as a cup lid. Trim the opening and scoop out the seeds.

2 Soak dried black mushrooms in warm water until soft, remove the stems and shred. Wash lily buds (ref. P. 28), soak in water until soft, then tie into knots. Shred both bamboo shoots and wood ears.

3 Heat a wok, add $^1/_2$ T. oil and heat. Stir-fry black mushrooms until fragrant. Add **2** and stock; bring to a boil. Pour the soup into pumpkin cup and cover with cup lid. Steam in a large steamer until tender (about 50 minutes). Season with **1**. Serve.

檸汁香梨 · Pear Salad

西洋梨（圖一）......... 2個　　香菜末..................... 1 小匙
洋蔥末、青椒末各1 大匙　　┌檸檬汁 .... 1 小匙
1┤
　　　　　　　　　　　　└鹽、麻油 ..... 各¼小匙

2 .... pears (illus.1)
1T. each:minced onion, minced green bell pepper
1 t. minced coriander

1┤ 1 t. .... lemon juice
¼ t. each:sesame oil, salt

1 西洋梨去皮去籽後，將梨肉切成小塊。
2 取梨肉、洋蔥末、青椒末、香菜末及**1**料拌勻即可。

■ 西洋梨可以蘋果或煮熟的馬鈴薯取代。

1 Pare the pears, remove the seeds and dice.
2 Toss diced pears, minced onions, minced green pepper, minced coriander and**1** together and serve.

■Pears maybe replaced by apples or boiled potatoes.

1

蘋果鬆 • Apple in Lettuce Wrapper

蘋果 280公克	西生菜 12片		
西洋芹菜 90公克	鹽 .... ¹/₂小匙		
荸薺 70公克	**1** 水 4杯		
葡萄乾 30公克	鹽 1大匙		
粉絲（見23頁）.. 15公克			

10 oz.(280 g)   apples
3¹/₄oz.(90 g) .... celery
2¹/₂oz.(70 g) .... water chestnuts
1 oz.(30 g) ...... raisins

¹/₂oz.(15 g) .... bean threads (ref. P. 23)
12 leaves ....lettuce
¹/₂ t. .... salt
1 4 C. .... water
1 T. .... salt

1 蘋果去皮切小丁，入 **1** 料中浸泡3分鐘瀝乾水份；西洋芹菜洗淨去老纖維後亦切小丁；荸薺洗淨去皮切碎；西生菜洗淨剪成直徑約10公分圓片備用。

2 鍋熱入油1杯燒至八分熱（180℃），入粉絲，隨即翻面撈起，瀝油後放在盤子上並壓碎。

3 鍋熱入油1大匙燒熱，入西洋芹菜、荸薺、鹽拌炒數下，再入蘋果丁、葡萄乾拌炒均勻，起鍋置冬粉上，再用西生菜包捲食用即可。

■ 為增加脆度，可以加一些切碎的油條。

1 Pare the apples and dice, soak in **1** for 3 minutes and drain. Wash celery and remove the tough fibers, dice. Wash the water chestnuts, pare and mince. Wash the lettuce leaves and trim into 10 cm (4") diameter circles.

2 Heat a wok, add 1 C. oil and heat to 180ºC (356ºF). Fry the bean threads on both sides, remove immediately and drain. Place the bean threads on a plate and crush to small pieces.

3 Heat a wok, add 1 T. oil and heat ; stir-fry celery, water chestnuts, and salt for a while. Add diced apples and raisins; mix well. Remove and place on top of the bean threads. Spoon a portion of the apple mixture into a lettuce leaf, wrap and serve.

■ Chopped fried Chinese cruller may be added to enhance the texture.

蘋果泡菜 · Pickled Apples

蘋果 250公克		┌ 白醋 5大匙
小黃瓜 225公克		│ 細砂糖 4大匙
白蘿蔔、胡蘿蔔	❶	│ 白胡椒粉 1小匙
.... 各150公克		└ 蒜末 1/2小匙
鹽 1大匙		

8³/₄oz.(250 g) apples
8 oz.(225 g) gherkin cucumbers
1/₃ lb.(150 g)each: carrots, turnips
1 T. .... salt

┌ 5 T. .... white vinegar
│ 4 T. ... granulated sugar
❶ 1 t. white pepper powder
│ 1/₂ t. .... minced garlic cloves └

1 蘋果、胡蘿蔔、白蘿蔔均去皮與小黃瓜都切小丁備用。

2 胡蘿蔔、白蘿蔔以鹽拌勻醃30分鐘，入小黃瓜丁拌勻續醃5分鐘後，入開水洗淨瀝乾備用。

3 將所有材料與❶料拌勻置冰箱醃泡一天即可。

1 Pare apples, carrots, and turnips; dice all. Dice gherkin cucumbers.

2 Marinate carrots and turnips with salt for 30 minutes first. Then add diced gherkin cucumbers. Mix well and marinate 5 more minutes. Rinse off the salt and pat dry.

3 Marinate all ingredients in ❶, refrigerate for one day. Serve.

青花白玉捲 · Jaded Rice Noodle Rolls

河粉（2片）...... 250公克		
青花菜 225公克		
蘆筍 110公克		
1 ⎡ 素火腿、熟筍 各65公克		
⎣ 香菇 8朵		
2 ⎡ 水 1大匙		
⎣ 太白粉 1小匙		

3 ⎡ 高湯 .... ¹/₂杯
⎜ 麻油 1大匙
⎜ 醬油、糖、酒、美極
⎜ 鮮味露 各1小匙
⎜ 鹽 .... ¹/₂小匙
⎣ 胡椒粉 .... ¹/₈小匙

8³/₄oz.(250 g) .... 2 flat
rice noodle sheets
8 oz.(225 g) broccoli
4 oz.(110 g) asparagus
1 ⎡ 2¹/₄oz.(65 g)each:
⎜ vegetarian ham,
⎜ boiled bamboo shoots
⎜ 8 .... dried
⎣ black mushrooms

2 ⎡ 1 T. .... water
⎣ 1 t. ..... cornstarch

3 ⎡ ¹/₂ C. .... stock
⎜ 1 T. .... sesame oil
⎜ 1 t. each:soy sauce,
⎜ suger,cooking wine,
⎜ Maggie sauce
⎜ ¹/₂ t. .... salt
⎣ ¹/₈ t. .... pepper

1 青花菜去老纖維後切小朵，入鍋燙熟後排盤圍邊，蘆
  筍入鍋川燙1分鐘取出漂涼；香菇泡軟洗淨去蒂，**1**
  料切絲，兩者均分成8等份。

2 河粉每片攤開切成四片，將一份**1**料及蘆筍置於河粉
  上包捲成圓柱狀，再一切為二，全部作好後入鍋蒸6
  分鐘即為白玉捲，最後將白玉捲置於青花菜中央。

3 **3**料煮開以**2**料勾芡，淋於白玉捲上即可。

1 Remove the tough broccoli fibers and cut into
  small sprigs, boil until cooked and arrange at
  the outer circle of a plate. Parboil the asparagus
  for a minute and rinse under cold water to cool.
  Soak dried black mushrooms in warm water
  until soft, wash and discard the stems. Shred
  all ingredients in **1** , divide into 8 equal portions
  for filling.

2 Cut each rice noodle sheet into 4 sheets. Place
  one portion of the filling and asparagus on the
  sheet; roll into cylinder and cut in half. Repeat
  the process until all done. Steam for 6 minutes.
  Arrange the rolls in the center of the plate
  surrounded by the broccoli.

3 Bring **3** to a boil and thicken with **2** . Pour the
  sauce over the rice noodle rolls and serve.

苜蓿春捲 · Alfalfa Sprout Rolls

苜蓿芽（圖一）..80公克
春捲皮 6張
沙拉醬 4大匙

1┌花生粉、菜酥（見35
　│頁）................ 各¹/₃杯
　│細砂糖 .... ¹/₂小匙
　└胡椒粉 .... ¹/₄小匙

2³/₄oz.(80 g) ... alfalfa
sprouts
6 sheets .... egg roll
skin
4 T. .... mayonnaise

1┌¹/₃ C. each:peanut
　│powder, vegetable
　│crisp(tsai su)
　│(ref. P. 35)
　│¹/₂ t. ... granulated
　│sugar
　└¹/₄ t. .... pepper

1 苜蓿芽洗淨，**1**料調勻分成6份備用。

2 取春捲皮一張，上置一份**1**料，並舖上1¹/₂小匙沙拉
　醬，續置苜蓿芽一份，再包捲成春捲狀，接口以沙拉
　醬黏住即可。

1 Wash clover sprouts and divide into 6 portions.
Mix **1** and divide into 6 portions.

2 On egg roll skins, place a portion of **1**, 1¹/₂ t.
mayonnaise, and a portion of clover sprouts
on top. Roll it up as spring roll, seal the opening
with mayonnaise. Makes six. Serve.

1

海苔米糕 · Seaweed Rice Cakes

長糯米 300公克		
紫菜 2¹/₂張		
花生粉 .... 適量		

❷	開水 4大匙
	醬油膏 3大匙
	蒜末 .... ¹/₂大匙
	糖 1小匙

❶	水 .... ¹/₂杯
	酒 .... ¹/₂大匙
	鹽 .... ¹/₄小匙
	胡椒粉、味精............
	.... 各¹/₈小匙

$10^1/_2$oz.(300 g) ... long grain glutinous rice

$2^1/_2$ sheets .... seaweed (nori)

as needed ...... peanut powder

❶	¹/₂ C. .... water
	¹/₂ T. cooking wine
	¹/₄ t. .... salt
	¹/₈ t. .... pepper

❷	4 T. .... water
	3 T. ...... thick soy sauce
	¹/₂ T. .... minced garlic cloves
	1 t. .... sugar

1 紫菜泡軟撈起瀝乾；糯米洗淨，泡水3～4小時後，瀝乾水份，再入❶料及紫菜拌勻，倒入舖有保鮮膜或玻璃紙的模型內，再入鍋蒸30分鐘，取出待涼切塊備用。

2 ❷料調勻即為沾料，取米糕沾上沾料，再沾上花生粉即可。

1 Soak seaweed sheets in water until soft, drain. Wash and soak the rice for 3 to 4 hours, drain. Mix rice with ❶ and seaweed. Pour the rice mixture into a cellophane paper lined mold. Steam for 30 minutes. Remove and leave to cool. Cut the rice cake into serving pieces.

2 Mix ❷ well for dipping sauce. Dip a piece of rice cake into the dipping sauce. Then roll in the peanut powder to coat. Serve.

步步高升 · Stir-fried Rice Cakes

寧波年糕（圖一）..........
.... 350公克
雪裡紅 120公克
熟綠竹筍 80公克
香菇 15公克

┌ 水 1/2杯
│ 酒 1大匙
1 胡椒粉、鹽、味精 ....
│ 各1/4小匙
└

12¹/₃oz.(350 g) ... Nin-Po rice cakes (illus.1)
4¹/₄oz.(120 g) ....
salted mustard greens
2³/₄oz.(80 g) .... boiled
green bamboo shoots

¹/₂oz.(15 g) .... dried
black mushrooms

┌ ¹/₂ C. .... water
│ 1 T. cooking wine
1 ¹/₄ t. each:pepper,
└ salt

1 年糕切片泡冷水備用，香菇泡軟洗淨去蒂與竹筍均切
  絲；雪裡紅切小丁備用。
2 鍋熱入油2大匙燒熱，入香菇爆香，續入雪裡紅、筍
  炒熟，再入瀝乾的年糕及**1**料以小火燜煮至湯汁剩1
  大匙（約3分鐘）即可。

1 Slice the rice cakes and soak in cold water.
  Soak the dried black mushrooms in warm
  water, wash and remove the stems; shred.
  Shred bamboo shoots. Dice salted mustard
  greens.
2 Heat a wok, add 2 T. oil and heat. Stir-fry
  shredded black mushrooms until fragrant. Add
  salted mustard greens and bamboo shoots
  until tender. Add drained rice cake slices and
  1 ; stir-fry over low heat until the sauce reduces
  to 1 T. (about 3 minutes). Serve.

1

滷香蒟蒻 · Soy Braised Shirataki

蒟蒻（見67頁） 360公克
麻油 1小匙
老薑 3片

1
┌ 紅辣椒 2條
│ 紅蔥頭末、蒜末 ....
└ 各1¹/₂小匙

2
┌ 醬油 6¹/₂大匙
│ 冰糖 4大匙
└ 鹽 1¹/₃小匙

3
┌ 八角 1朵
│ 花椒、小茴香 ....
│ .... 各²/₃小匙
└ 甘草、桂皮 各2片

$12^2/_3$ oz.(360 g) ....
shirataki (ref. P. 67)
1 t. .... sesame oil
3 slices .. ginger root

1
┌ 2 red chili peppers
│ $1^1/_2$ t. each: minced
│ red shallots, minced
└ garlic cloves

2
┌ $6^1/_2$ T. .. soy sauce
│ 4 T. crystal sugar
└ $1^1/_3$ t. .... salt

3
┌ 1 ....star anise
│ $^2/_3$ t. each:
│ Szechwan pepper
│ corns, fennels
│ 2 slices each:
└ licorice, cinnamon

1 紅辣椒切末，鍋熱入油4大匙燒熱，入 **1** 料爆香，再入 **2** 料煮開即為蔥油料。

2 **3** 料裝入滷包袋中，加水4杯煮開，續入薑片煮30分鐘後，再入蔥油料續煮30分鐘即為滷汁。

3 蒟蒻洗淨切成八等份，每份再切成2片後，從中間劃一刀（圖一），翻轉（圖二）成麻花狀，入滷汁中滷20分鐘，撈起撒上麻油即可。

1 Mince red chili peppers. Heat a wok, add 4 T. oil and heat. Stir-fry **1** until fragrant. Add **2**, bring to a boil. This is the shallot sauce.

2 Sew **3** into a spice bag. Add 4 C. water and bring to a boil. Add ginger slices and boil for 30 minutes. Add shallot sauce and continue cooking for 30 minutes to make braising sauce.

3 Wash shirataki and cut into 8 equal portions. Then cut each piece in half. Slit the center (illus.1) of each piece, then turn the center slit outward (illus.2) to form a twisted opening. Cook shirataki twists in braising sauce for 20 minutes. Sprinkle on sesame oil and serve.

1

2

酸菜蒟蒻絲 · Sesame Shirataki

酸菜、蒟蒻絲（圖一）..
.... 各150公克
熟白芝麻 1小匙

1┌ 蒜末、薑末 .. 各1小匙
　└ 紅辣椒 1枝

2┌ 水 1/4杯
　│ 醬油 1 1/2大匙
　│ 糖 2小匙
　│ 酒 1小匙
　│ 味精 1/4小匙
　└ 胡椒粉 1/8小匙

1/3 lb.(150 g)each:
sour mustard,
shredded shirataki
(illus.1)
1 t. ..... roasted white
sesame seeds

1┌ 1 t. each:　minced
　│ garlic cloves,
　│ minced ginger roots
　└ 1　red chili pepper

2┌ 1/4 C. .... water
　│ 1 1/2 T. .. soy sauce
　│ 2 t. .... sugar
　│ 1 t.　cooking wine
　└ 1/8 t. .... pepper

1 辣椒去籽與酸菜均洗淨切絲，鍋內入水3杯煮開，續入蒟蒻絲煮3分鐘取出漂涼，切段備用。

2 鍋熱入油2大匙燒熱，入 **1** 料爆香，續入蒟蒻絲及 **2** 料煮3分鐘，再入酸菜絲拌炒均勻取出，最後撒上熟白芝麻即可。

1 Remove the seeds from red chili pepper, wash and shred. Shred sour mustard. Bring 3 C. water to a boil, parboil shredded shirataki for 3 minutes; rinse under cold water to cool, then cut into sections.

2 Heat a wok, add 2 T. oil and heat. Stir-fry **1** until fragrant. Add shredded shirataki and **2**, cook for 3 minutes. Mix in shredded sour mustard. Sprinkle on roasted white sesame seeds. Serve.

1

軟脆夾香 · Tofu Skin Rolls in Crepes

麵粉	300公克		醬油	1大匙
香菇	28公克	**1**	糖	1小匙
豆皮	3張		水	3杯
熱開水	1杯	**2**	甜麵醬	2大匙
蔥末	5大匙		糖	2¹/₂小匙
麻油	2小匙	**3**	麵粉、水	各1¹/₂大匙

10¹/₂oz.(300 g) .... all purpose flour

1 oz.(28 g) .... dried black mushrooms

3 sheets .... bean curd skin

1 C. .... hot water

5 T. ..... minced green onions

2 t. .... sesame oil

1 ⌈ 1 T. ...... soy sauce
　 ⌊ 1 t. .... sugar

2 ⌈ 3 C. .... water
　 ⌈ 2 T. .... sweet bean paste
　 ⌊ 2¹/₂ t. .... sugar

3 ⌈ 1¹/₂ T. each: all purpose flour, water

1 香菇泡軟洗淨去蒂切絲，香菇水留用。鍋熱入油1大匙燒熱，入香菇炒香，再入半杯香菇水及**1**料炒至湯汁收乾，撈起分成3等份；**2**料煮開待涼備用。

2 麵粉過篩，加熱開水拌勻後揉成均勻且光滑的麵糰，分成20等份。每份麵糰用手壓扁後，表面均勻抹上一層麻油，取兩塊麵糰合在一起（圖一），用擀麵棍擀成直徑12公分之薄皮，放入燒熱的平底鍋中，以小火乾烙至兩面變色且膨發後，取出一分為二即為麵皮。

3 取一張豆皮攤開，將一份香菇絲鋪成8公分寬但比豆皮稍短之長條狀（圖二），再將多出之豆皮往內摺上（圖三），接口處以**3**料黏住即為豆皮捲。其餘兩捲依此作法捲好。

4 鍋熱入油2大匙燒熱，入豆皮捲煎至兩面呈金黃色且酥脆，取出每份切7塊，即為豆皮酥。

5 取一張麵皮，塗上**2**料，撒上蔥末，放一塊豆皮酥再捲成長條狀即可。

1 Soak dried black mushrooms in warm water until soft, remove the stems and shred; retain the soaking water for later use. Heat a wok, add 1T. oil and heat, stir-fry the black mushrooms until fragrant. Add half cup soaking water and **1** ; cook until the sauce is completely evaporated. Remove and divide into 3 portions. Bring **2** to a boil and leave to cool.

2 Sift the flour, add hot water and knead into smooth dough. Divide the dough into 20 equal portions. Press each portion flat and brush on a layer of sesame oil. Press two dough portions together gently (illus.1) and roll into a 12cm (4¹/₂") diameter thin crepe. Fry the crepe on a heated dry pan over low heat, until the crepe turns light brown on both sides and puffs up. Remove the crepe from the pan. The crepe should be easily separated to two, one-side-browned crepes. Repeat the process until all crepes are made.

3 Spread a sheet of bean curd skin out. Arrange a portion of shredded black mushrooms into a 8 cm (3") wide long strip, a little shorter then bean curd skin (illus.2). Fold the bean curd skin over (illus.3) and seal the opening with **3**. Make three rolls.

4 Heat a wok, add 2 T. oil and heat. Fry the rolls until golden on both sides and crispy. Remove and cut into seven pieces.

5 Brush **2** on a crepe and sprinkle on minced green onion, then a piece of tofu roll; roll the crepe up and serve.

1

2

3

六人份 SERVES 6

壽　司 · Sushi Rolls

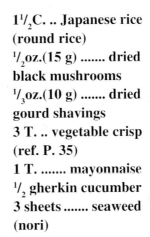
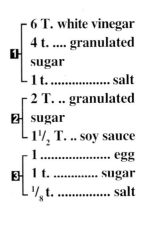

蓬萊米 1¹/₂杯		白醋 6大匙	
香菇 15公克	**❶**	細砂糖 4小匙	
干瓢 10公克		鹽 1小匙	
菜酥（見35頁）....3大匙		細砂糖 2大匙	
沙拉醬 1大匙	**❷**	醬油 1¹/₂大匙	
小黃瓜 .... ¹/₂條		蛋 1個	
紫菜 3張	**❸**	糖 1小匙	
		鹽 .... ¹/₈小匙	

1¹/₂ C. .. Japanese rice (round rice)
¹/₂ oz.(15 g) .... dried black mushrooms
¹/₃ oz.(10 g) .... dried gourd shavings
3 T. .. vegetable crisp (ref. P. 35)
1 T. .... mayonnaise
¹/₂ gherkin cucumber
3 sheets .... seaweed (nori)

❶
6 T. white vinegar
4 t. .... granulated sugar
1 t. .... salt

❷
2 T. .. granulated sugar
1¹/₂ T. .. soy sauce

❸
1 .... egg
1 t. .... sugar
¹/₈ t. .... salt

1 米洗淨瀝乾加水1¹/₂杯，入鍋煮成飯後，取出趁熱拌入❶料並打鬆吹涼再分成3份。

2 干瓢洗淨加水煮至軟（約10分鐘）取出，小黃瓜切成3條備用。

3 香菇泡軟洗淨去蒂，泡香菇水1杯留用，加干瓢入香菇水及❷料煮開後，改小火煮20分鐘，取出待涼，香菇切絲，兩者均分成3份備用。

4 ❸料調勻。鍋熱取紗布沾油塗在鍋子上，入蛋液煎至半凝固即折成長條狀，再續煎至熟並切成3份備用。

5 紫菜置於竹簾上（圖一），取一份白飯舖於紫菜上，再放上一份香菇、干瓢、蛋、小黃瓜、菜酥、沙拉醬（圖二），捲成壽司，其餘2份作法相同，每條再切成8塊即可。

■ 壽司形狀可依各人喜好做變化。

1 Add 1¹/₂ C. water to rice and cook until done. While warm, mix ❶ into rice and loosen the rice. Leave to cool and divide into three portions.

2 Wash dried gourd shavings and boil in water until tender (about 10 minutes). Drain. Cut the gherkin cucumber into 3 long strips.

3 Wash and soak dried black mushrooms in water until soft, remove the stems and retain 1C. of the soaking water for later use. Cook gourd shavings with mushroom soaking water and ❷, bring to a boil. Turn the heat to low and simmer over low heat for 20 minutes. Remove and leave to cool. Shred the black mushrooms. Divide both into 3 portions.

4 Heat a pan, brush with a thin film of oil, fry well mixed ❸. When the egg mixture is half set, fold it to form a long strip; cook until solidly set. Cut it into 3 equal strips.

5 On a bamboo screen roller (illus.1), place a sheet of seaweed, spread a portion of rice, gherkin cucumber, egg, mayonnaise, vegetable crisp, gourd shavings and shredded black mushrooms (illus.2). Roll up tightly. Repeat and make two more rolls. Cut each roll into 8 pieces.

■Variations of sushi can be created as you like.

1

2

純青出版社

劃撥帳號：12106299
電　　話：(〇二)五〇八四三三一
傳　　真：(〇二)五〇七四九〇二
地　　址：台北市松江路125號 5 樓

健康食譜
- 100道菜
- 120頁
- 中英對照

Healthful Cooking
- 100 recipes
- 120 pages
- Chinese/English Bilingual

素食
- 84道菜
- 120頁
- 中英對照

Vegetarian Cooking
- 84 recipes
- 120 pages
- Chinese/English Bilingual

微波食譜第一冊
- 62道菜
- 112頁
- 中英對照

Microwave Cooking Chinese Style
- 62 recipes
- 112 pages
- Chinese/English Bilingual

微波食譜第二冊
- 76道菜
- 128頁
- 中英對照

Microwave Cooking Chinese Style 2
- 76 recipes
- 128 pages
- Chinese/English Bilingual

飲茶食譜
- 88道菜
- 128頁
- 中英對照

Chinese Dim Sum
- 88 recipes
- 128 pages
- Chinese/English Bilingual

美味小菜
- 92道菜
- 96頁
- 中英對照

Appetizers
- 92 recipes
- 96 pages
- Chinese/English Bilingual

實用烘焙
- 77道點心
- 96頁
- 中英對照

International Baking Delight
- 77 recipes
- 96 pages
- Chinese/English Bilingual

四川菜
- 115道菜
- 96頁
- 中英對照

Chinese Cuisine Szechwan Style
- 115 recipes
- 96 pages
- Chinese/English Bilingual

上海菜
- 91道菜
- 96頁
- 中英對照

Chinese Cuisine Shanghai Style
- 91 recipes
- 96 pages
- Chinese/English Bilingual

台灣菜
- 73道菜
- 120頁
- 中英對照

Chinese Cuisine Taiwanese Style
- 73 recipes
- 120 pages
- Chinese/English Bilingual

Chin-Chin Publishing

5th fl., 125 Sung Chiang Rd.,Taipei 104, Taiwan, R.O.C
Tel:(02)5084331 Fax:(02)5074902

麵食-家常篇
- 91道菜
- 96頁
- 中英對照

Noodles Home Cooking
- 91 recipes
- 96 pages
- Chinese/English Bilingual

麵食-精華篇
- 87道菜
- 96頁
- 中英對照

Noodles Classical Cooking
- 87 recipes
- 96 pages
- Chinese/English Bilingual

米食-家常篇
- 84道菜
- 96頁
- 中英對照

Rice Home Cooking
- 84 recipes
- 96 pages
- Chinese/English Bilingual

米食-傳統篇
- 82道菜
- 96頁
- 中英對照

Rice Traditional Cooking
- 82 recipes
- 96 pages
- Chinese/English Bilingual

家常100
- 100道菜
- 96頁
- 中英對照

Favorite Chinese Dishes
- 100 recipes
- 96 pages
- Chinese/English Bilingual

養生藥膳
- 73道菜
- 128頁
- 中英對照

Chinese Herb Cooking for Health
- 73 recipes
- 128 pages
- Chinese/English Bilingual

健康素
- 76道菜
- 96頁
- 中英對照

Simply Vegetarian
- 76 recipes
- 96 pages
- Chinese/English Bilingual

營養便當
- 147道菜
- 96頁
- 中文版

嬰幼兒食譜
- 140道菜
- 104頁
- 中文版

家常菜
- 226道菜
- 200頁
- 中文版

庖廚偏方　庖廚錦囊　庖廚樂
- 中文版

味全家政班

Wei-Chuan Cooking School

味全家政班創立於民國五十年，經過三十餘年的努力，它不只是國內歷史最悠久的家政研習班，更成爲一所正式學制之外的專門學校。

創立之初，味全家政班以教授中國菜及研習烹飪技術爲主，因教學成果良好，備受各界讚譽，乃於民國五十二年，增闢插花、工藝、美容等各門專科，精湛的師資，教學內容的充實，深獲海內外的肯定與好評。

三十餘年來，先後來班參與研習的學員已近二十萬人次，學員的足跡遍及台灣以外，更有許多國外的團體或個人專程抵台，到味全家政班求教，在習得中國菜烹調的精髓後，或返回居住地經營餐飲業，或擔任家政教師，或獲聘爲中國餐廳主廚者大有人在，成就倍受激賞。

近年來，味全家政班亟力研究開發改良中國菜餚，並深入國際間，採集各種精緻、道地美食，除了樹立中華文化「食的精神」外，並將各國烹飪口味去蕪存菁，擷取地方特色。爲了確保這些研究工作更加落實，我們特將這些集合海內外餐飲界與研發單位的精典之作，以縝密的拍攝技巧與專業編輯，出版各式食譜，以做傳承。

薪傳與發揚中國烹飪的藝術，是味全家政班一貫的理念，日後，也將秉持宗旨，永續不輟。

Since its establishment in 1961, Wei-Chuan Cooking School has made a continuous commitment toward improving and modernizing the culinary art of cooking and special skills training. As a result, it is the oldest and most successful school of its kind in Taiwan.

In the beginning, Wei-Chuan Cooking School was primarily teaching and researching Chinese cooking techniques. However, due to popular demand, the curriculum was expanded to cover courses in flower arrangements, handcrafts, beauty care, dress making and many other specialized fields by 1963.

The fact that almost 200,000 students, from Taiwan and other countries all over the world, have matriculated in this school can be directly attributed to the high quality of the teaching staff and the excellent curriculum provided to the students. Many of the graduates have become successful restaurant owners and chefs and in numerous cases, respected teachers.

While Wei-Chuan Cooking School has always been committed to developing and improving Chinese cuisine, we have recently extended our efforts toward gathering information and researching recipes from different provinces of China. With the same dedication to accuracy and perfection as always, we have begun to publish these authentic regional gourmet recipes for our devoted readers. These new publications will continue to reflect the fine tradition of quality our public has grown to appreciate and expect.